Irina Vujaklija

365 and more.
Stories from
A Thinking Bond Blonde

AF368216

Book collaborators:

Lecturers and editors:
Marija Pavlovic and Sam Kennett

Illustrations:
Magda Radojlovic

Print preparation:
Dejan Ristic

365 and more.
Stories from
A Thinking Bond Blonde

Irina Vujaklija

This book has an intention, or it is better to say that my intention is to make you think more, to question everything, your beliefs, your intentions. To inspire you to take action.. to live, to love..
It is dedicated to all those who need that extra boost, to all those who feel like they don't belong here, to all who feel lost and to all who struggle. This means all of you, because these are situations and emotions that we all face throughout the life.

We live in a world where people have become robots, imitating each other. The world of superficial values and superficial people. We been taught to live up to other people's expectations, yet no one has taught us to love ourselves. We've been taught to serve others, yet no one taught us to take care of ourselves. It sounds like slavery.

Every step I have made, has brought me to here, where I am now. I have way too many experiences that I would like to share with you. My intention is to motivate, to help and to share my thoughts based on my experience and my life situations.

So, if you feel like you belong here, fasten your seat belt and enjoy the ride. I will try to explain through a series of short stories my view and my perspective. Speaking about serious subjects but not in a dramatic way. Because that's what life is.. not time for drama. You should enjoy life and not take it too seriously, no matter what happens. I hope that you are going to feel comfortable and have the sensation that you're talking (listening :D) to me, like talking to a friend while drinking some coffee. And, yes.. pardon my French in advance.

Now.. it's time to enjoy, please, have fun reading it!

Namaste,

Irina Vujaklija

1

"Don't let my honesty offend you."

That's just me being honest about everything. It's simply my perspective, so why be offended?

And no... I'm not talking about senseless opinions, the insulting ones, judging others and all that blah blah blah stuff.

My honesty is my truth. My way of being. My life. I will always give my opinion if someone asks me to... I will always say what I think, I won't just say things others would like to hear.

I either attract strong minds or the weak ones.

Usually, the weak ones find my words offensive or aggressive or as "too much". Normally, they get triggered by them... so they usually attack me, and they often do it from my back.

But the thing is, I just like "straight-to-the-point" talks. I looove truth.

I prefer honesty, no matter what. No matter how difficult it seems. That's why I like and respect people who tell me the truth, no matter the reaction. It's up to me how will I deal with it. Just tell me the fucking truth. A lot of people prefer to live a lie.

None of my business. The one who doesn't respect my words and my opinion, my life, my perspective... That person simply can't be part of my life.

And I believe that is a kind of a mutual thing.

2

"People who defend your name when you're not around are the most loyal friends you could ever get."

People with integrity!!! People should learn what loyalty and integrity mean! And act accordingly.

I'm not interested in how nice you are when you are talking to me, I'm more concerned with who you are and what you speak behind my back!!! Because my friend's loyalty shouldn't depend on my presence!

As we grow up, we (should) realize that it's more important to have real friends than tones of fake ones.

Surround yourself with people who positively feed your soul, heart & mind. Do you have people who are "toxic" for you, but you still hang out with them, calling them friends? Why?

It's not selfish to protect yourself, your energy. It means that you have grown up, that you are aware and conscious about your choices. It's self-love, self-respect and it's very wise! It's your life and your precious time we talk about here...

People come and go. That's life.

Thus, remember:

There is nothing wrong with letting go of anyone who doesn't make you feel good about yourself.

The same way around... There is nothing wrong when someone lets you go because you were not making them feel good about themselves.

You are not the centre of the Universe!!!

Analyse yourself the same way you analyse others.

So... before you feed your wishes and expectations... remember that life doesn't work that way, my friend... Before you ask for anything, make sure that you also give back the same. It has to be mutual... what you give and put out there, you will receive it back.

3

It's never too late.

Someone has taught us that when you reach a certain age, it's usually late for changes...

If you want one "happy" life (happy by your own definition), you should destroy that belief!

IT'S NEVER TOO LATE AND YOU'RE NEVER TOO OLD:

- to start again

- to change your life

- to change your job

- to do things right

- to FALL IN LOVE

- to be whoever you want to be

- to change things

- to learn

- to follow your dreams

- to move to another country

and so on and so forth...

Aaaaand of course, those who say (to themselves or to others) that it's too late, this one is for you especially: It's never too late to shut up and mind your own fucking business! If you don't want to change your life, fine, just don't discourage others from doing it!

Time for action is always: Now!

4

"Grandpa: "A real loser is someone who's so afraid of not winning he doesn't even try." Little Miss Sunshine (2006)"

Courage is not the absence of fear! Courage is going on in spite of the fear you feel.

Being a loser is so easy… giving up is so easy… that's how most people live nowadays…

But to stand up for yourself, for your dreams, for the life you dream of… no matter how many times you have failed, no matter how many people will judge you… Oh, that's what bravery is!

That's how you become a hero, when you conquer all your "demons". Demons within you and around you.

5

"99% of things you worry about never happens."

Being afraid, worrying and overthinking – that's nothing but the stream of your negative thoughts…

It's the 'maybes' and 'what-ifs' that will kill you.

Oh, what if I fail?

But, darling what if you succeed?

A huge difference, right? Makes you wonder: why is it easier to think negatively?

6

"When you apologize, there is one rule that you must follow: you must promise to do things differently next time."

A changed behaviour is the only true apology!

When someone hurts you, and you tell them... of course, that person should apologize!

But... is that enough? Of course not! What's the purpose of the apology if the person keeps doing what they're sorry for? I think there is a medical term for that condition... And I would call it a C.NT But, seriously now. Think about it. What's that? A lack of respect, interest, trust? What's the motive of this person to hurt you over and over again (if you allow it and let it happen over and over again, of course, that's also a lack of self-respect). People can make a mistake once, but the next time they do it, it's a matter of choice. They are conscious about it. And you are too by forgiving them the same thing all over again. (And vice versa)

Of course, these people will keep hurting you if you allow something like that. We teach others how to treat us, by what we allow as well.

Understanding this is a crucial thing for change. (That's how we develop emotional intelligence and empathy)

Aaaand the most important thing is that this also applies to you if you apologize without really meaning it.

The golden rule is:

Jim Jefferies: "The bible should be one sheet of paper, and on that paper, it should say: Try not to be a cunt, and if you do that every day, you'll be a good person."

And if you're sensitive, then *pardon my French*.

If you want to fly you have to let go of things that weigh you down.

7

"The importance of letting go..."

Your heart should be calm, your vision clear, you should be at peace with your past, so you can be at peace with where you're heading to.

Maybe not everything will feel just right from the outside, as it probably never will. But from within – it should definitely feel so. And that's the only thing that matters!

The importance of letting go and making peace with your past is crucial. Forgiving people, forgiving yourself and moving on. Forgiving others doesn't mean you're accepting their behaviour, it simply means you understand it.

8

"Isn't it heavy to carry your past on your shoulders?"

Make peace with your past (learn how to accept, forgive and let go...) & don't bring it to your present, because that will definitely reflect on your future.

9

"You need to destroy the idea that there's an expectation to do things by a certain age. You don't have to be married with kids at 25. It's okay to not have your dream job at 30 or to not have graduated by 22. There are no rules to life. Life is neither a race, nor a competition."

Today is a perfect day for self-reflection and requestioning one's beliefs, don't you think?

Today, I will make you think for a bit. (I know, I know...)

But in order to help you, I will start by asking you a simple question: Do you feel the pressure that society puts on us?

If you do, then you need to fight back. YOU need to be the one who chooses what's good for you. YOU need to make decisions that will lead you into a peaceful and fulfilled life.

The first rule is: Do not feel guilty if you don't fit other people's beliefs, expectations or plans they have for you!

You are here to live your own life and make your own unique positive influence in the world.

It's perfectly OK if you don't want to have kids.

It's perfectly OK if you don't want to get married.

It's perfectly OK to get divorced if your marriage makes you unhappy.

It's perfectly OK to let go of anything that is toxic for you.

It's perfectly OK to move on.

It's perfectly OK to be successful in the sense of what success means to you alone.

Success was never about money or titles anyway. Success is simply leading a meaningful and fulfilled life. Whether you are a taxi driver, a housewife, a doctor, you name it, it doesn't matter. These are just words and titles. YOU ARE NOT YOUR JOB. Your job does not represent who you are. Your job is not a measurement of the quality of your life.

So, stop torturing yourself by comparing your life to the life of others!

And please, stop listening to the messages sent through media.

They are the most dangerous venom. Do not let them influence YOUR life. Nobody knows better than you what makes you happy and what is good for you.

Set yourself free.

10

You probably know the saying: *"Time heals all wounds."*

We all know that is NOT true.

Time doesn't heal anything, it simply teaches us how to live with the pain inflicted.

How many times have you heard this advice?

Whenever we are hurt for whatever reason someone will try to comfort us by saying: time will heal your wounds.

Well, it won't.

The same goes when we lose someone. people will again say: time heals everything.

Well, it doesn't.

What is time anyway? Such a relative term.

Time won't heal anything unless you help yourself in the process.

Learning how to accept things just the way they are is crucial. Of course, in the healing process you need to give yourself some time. But you also need to let all emotions go through you. You need to cry, feel sad, frustrated, in pain etc. Only then will you accept the things you can't change and move on.

Pain is an inevitable part of our lives. That's why we must learn to accept, live with it and move on with it.

11

"A healthy mind does not speak ill of others."

Know this: People who are satisfied with their lives don't go around destroying, insulting or bullying others.

These kinds of attackers are especially "brave" on social media. No guts in "real" life, but *hell yes* in the virtual one. Behind their screens. That's very miserable if you ask me.

There is probably something that hurt them deep inside, and they think they will feel better about themselves if they make you feel bad as well.

Oh, how wrong... They are not even aware that they will only feel worse after. So, if you are one of their victims... try not to be "infected" with their frustrations.

And again, the most important thing – if you feel any kind of frustration (we all deal with a great amount of stress), don't be that cunt going around spreading your sh.t. Find what bothers you and confront your problems like a real man or woman.

Pardon my French... It's me again, just being explicitly honest. As usual.

12

"Never belong to a crowd; Never belong to a nation; Never belong to a religion; Never belong to a race. Belong to the whole existence. Why limit yourself to small things? When the whole is available." Osho

Why would you put a label on yourself and why would you limit yourself?

Just be yourself (people very often understand this in a very superficial way).

Just because you are from the USA, Spain, Serbia or any other country... this doesn't mean that you are better than anybody else. This doesn't make you a good person.

Religion??? I mean... I'm laughing really hard now... It is invented to divide people... the only true religion should be LOVE. So, listen to you heart! Have faith and believe in yourself.

Race? I mean really? Look at a panda – it's both black and white and it's from Asia. And sooooo adorable.

Why limit yourself when there is a world full of undiscovered beauty out there.

13

"Be a better you, for you."

Whatever you do... do it for yourself!

I see very often quotes like: Do it for the people who want to see you fail!

Well no! I disagree strongly. I know that there are very nasty people all around us, I know this all tooooo well (first of all, make sure you are not one of them – it's time for self-analysis).

But no... That would be a completely wrong intention. They shouldn't be your focus. Yes, you can use them as a fuel, as some lessons that will help you be stronger. And that's it.

Do it for yourself. You deserve it, ok? To be a better person, to feel good, to do good, to succeed in your goals (whatever they might be).

And:

Don't preach what you don't practice.

14

"I like when I don't have to be careful about what I say. That's when you know you are with the right people."

That was something I had to learn the hard way... You know, this blondie likes to express herself and wants to be understood perfectly. As I'm so transparent and direct, I've always wondered how come someone doesn't understand me.

BUT... That's not how life works.

If I don't need to be careful with what I say (be it stupid or not), that means that I'm with the right people (for me). If I can simply be myself, oh then, that's my tribe.

If I have to translate my thoughts or feel awkward after saying something... That's not my tribe. Or even worse, if I need to translate my humour! Oh, my God! And I do have the tendency to make jokes about everything.

That one would be a sign for a bye-bye.

15

"The less you respond to negative people, the more peaceful your life will become."

The empty vessel makes the loudest sound.

It's just an echo of their frustrations and emptiness.

Know that when ignorance speaks and when you have to deal with negative people, the only thing that matters is to keep your inner peace.

Sometimes this can be veeeery challenging but one has to learn when to stay quiet... in order to stay healthy.

16

"You can if you think you can!"

Those who think they can, and those who think they can't... are both usually right. It's up to you to choose the side.

17

"You can't open up the story of my life and just fucking go to page 738 and think you know me."

Still, people think they do. But they are wrong.

I'm very open (communicative), yet a very private person.

Usually all people judge others from their own perspective. Based on what I allow them to see.

Therefore...

Next time you think that you know someone, simply ask yourself do you REALLY know that person?

And if you don't... there is always a way to get to know someone you are interested in. But what is veeeeery important: it must be mutual!

18

"Have you ever gone out of your way to help someone and found out how ungrateful they are?"

Way too many times!

I'm sure we have all experienced similar situations.

The thing is: this shouldn't stop you from helping others!

If they are ungrateful, this tells something about them, not about you!

If you are willing to help others, you do that simply because you want to help and not because you expect anything in return... and if you do, then you're not helping but doing some business. Noooot nice.

And it's even worse if you have helped someone and afterwards rubbed it in their face. THESE THINGS DEFINE YOU.

Again, that's not help.

So, don't worry about whether people are being grateful or not, help them simply because you want to help!

That's the only thing that matters.

19

"A wise man makes his own decisions; an ignorant man follows public opinion." A Chinese proverb.

Follow to follow?

Like for like?

Speaking about social media, do you like someone's post just because it already has so many likes or do you like it because you see real value in it and you really like it?

Do you buy something because you like it, or because it is a trend for this season?

Do you follow others because they have many followers, or because you can learn something from them?

Do you like something just because other people like it or because it resonates with your taste?

Do you belong to the crowd or you prefer walking your walk by yourself, even if it means walking alone?

Do you follow other people's opinions, or do you know how to stand up for yourself?

Do you accept other people's beliefs even if they don't resonate with you, or do you create your own beliefs?

Do you accept things and rules just because someone said you have to, or do you use your common sense to accept only those things that feel right for you?

Do you get offended by other people's opinions about you, or do you know who you are?

20

Soothsayer: "Your story may not have such a happy beginning, but that doesn't make you who you are. It is the rest of your story, who you *choose* to be." Kung Fu Panda 2 – 2011

Don't use excuses from the past that might hold you back and stop you from having one bright and great future.

Maybe you can't choose where you will be born, your childhood or your family (I say 'Maybe' because there are different theories about this matter, but they are not relevant for this post), but what you can choose is *now*. How you will live now. Where you will live now. Anything. You CAN choose. You CAN decide. And then, you CAN plan what to do and how to do it. You are in charge of your life. You are creator of your life. Remember this.

21

"It doesn't matter where I am; I'm yours."

Most people say distance is a reason enough to give up on someone, a genuine reason to end a relationship... and I'm like: oh, really?! Let me tell you something: No, it's not. I know, I know – it's mind blowing!

All these are just excuses... what if we say instead: Distance means nothing when someone means a lot. What if... distance is just a test to prove if your love is true and strong enough?

I would say that distance gives us a reason to love harder.

My home is where my heart is. Always! Distance is not for the fearful, it's for the bold!

22

"A wise man can always be found alone. A weak man can always be found in a crowd."

It is easy to be part of a crowd...

It takes true courage and strength to stand alone. To walk your journey alone.

When you are part of a crowd, you simply follow others and you follow the crowd's direction. You will never go further than the crowd. You will think the same as others think, and you will create YOUR beliefs accordingly. Your beliefs will then shape your life and your future.

That's how maaaany people live today.

If you walk your journey alone... you will learn so many things about yourself, about life and all those things you are interested in. You will never stop learning. You will broaden your horizons... This won't be easy, but it will be the right thing to do. For yourself. And although it's not so easy, it is SO WORTH IT.

This doesn't mean that you will not be part of any crowd. The big difference is that you will be able to choose and navigate your crowd. And actually, it won't be a crowd at all. You will choose "your tribe" and you'll choose it carefully.

23

"Always stand up for what you believe in... even if it means standing alone." - Kim Hanks

Speak up for yourself!
Stand up for yourself!
Stand up for what you believe in, for what is right, even if it means standing alone.

So if you think and believe that pineapple goes perfectly well on pizza, then enjoy your pizza! Don't let anyone tell you that it's not right. Not even me (and I do think that pineapple on pizza is a terrible idea).

Anyway... You know what I mean. Stand up for what is right... always!

This can be very challenging, but you have to (learn to) believe in yourself. Believe in your own power because that's how you will protect yourself and your dreams.

Thus, not only will you protect yourself, but you will also change the lives of others for the better. Be in charge of your life. Be responsible for your life.

And justice for pineapples. And for pizza.

"Everyone is trying to find the right person, but nobody is trying to be the right person."

Not everyone is like this, but far too many people are...

How strange is this, right? People are too demanding, always wanting something more, something better from others... Yet, how many of them ask themselves do they provide the same?

Wanting *more* and *better* is fine... BUT only as long as you give back the same.

Most often, people look for happiness in others, or look for others to complete them, and that's not how life works!

I always like to say: you only deserve the love you give!

Yeah, I know I'm good for you, but what makes you think that you are good for me?

What makes you think that you are the one I want to be with?

It's time for self-analysis. Always. Always start from yourself!

Do you want loyalty? Are you loyal?

Do you want respect? Do you respect your partner?

Do you want support? Are you supportive?

And so on...

Make sure that what you wish for is reciprocal with what you give. Because, you know, sometimes you will need much more support than usual, but don't forget that sometimes your partner will need the same.

25

"Growth is painful. Change is painful. But, nothing is as painful as staying stuck where you do not belong" - Mandy Hale

Oh, how true this is...

People stay in their comfort zones (no progress, no growth, no challenges) because they don't want to feel that painful process of growth...

They fear judgments. If they change, what will other people tell? How will other people react?

They avoid facing situations they don't feel good about so they can avoid... misunderstandings, possible loss of respect in other people's eyes, and so on, the list is endless.

In the end, it usually all comes to living up to other people's expectations (sometimes or often not even being aware of it).

SO, they decide to stay in their comfort zones living A PAINFUL life... and it's painful because they don't live the way they want to. They don't feel free. They suppress emotions. And all these things lead to other issues... and then they look for "remedies" to fix consequences instead of focusing on the problem's root.

Isn't it ironic? Don't you think?

26

"Avoiding an emotion doesn't heal it, it takes away the possibility of it being healed."

Suppressing your emotions can lead you to self-destruction.

We live in a world where the only solution to all your problems is: a smile.

Why the fuck would you smile if you want to cry?

Instead of listening to superficial understanding of life of so-called life coaches, try to listen to yourself for a change.

If you feel sad, then be it. Cry. Tears serve the purpose of letting go of negative emotions we build up within us. So, respect yourself and listen to your body and its needs.

All these are necessary steps you should take in order to feel good. You can't jump over them, suppressing or ignoring your emotions. No, no, no.

Self-acceptance is the key. Feel all emotions... there's nothing wrong with them and there's nothing to be embarrassed about simply being sad.

27

"Being in a relationship won't heal you and being single won't kill you"

Being in a relationship won't heal you neither will complete you...

Being in a relationship won't heal you neither will complete you...

If you understand that you are already complete and that other half is not there to complete you, then you will stop depending on them for accomplishing your fulfillness and happiness.

That's your job.

No one ever taught us how to love ourselves.

And that is the essential thing.

That's why it is so important to spend some time on your own.

This will help you learn so much about yourself.

You will understand that solitude can bring you more joy than being in a relationship that doesn't make you happy.

You will learn to be your own best friend.

You will learn to respect and value yourself.

You'll become open-minded.

You will set up standards so high that you won't allow yourself to shrink back just so that others can feel comfortable around you.

And so many other things...

But above all... you will learn what self-love is and you will be ready to love others and to receive love.

So, think again, what may "kill" you? Being single or being in a loveless relationship?

Being in a relationship will never complete you. Neither will it heal you.

My math: 1+1=1

28

"No one in the world is perfect"

There is no such a thing as *perfect/perfection*. Society puts pressure upon us to live a perfect life, to look perfect to find somebody perfect... based on "their own" standards.

Please stop torturing yourself to be perfect or to live a perfect life according to others.

Define what perfect means to You! And stick to that. Whether we talk about yourself, your partner, life, job, name it... find what's perfect for You!

And be simply and perfectly you!

Keep in mind that what might be perfect for You, might not be perfect for others. So, respect other people's way of thinking and their definition of perfection.

And... Instead of looking for perfection, search for progress by learning from mistakes!

29

"Don't put the key to your happiness in someone else's pocket"

The only expectations you should live up to are the expectations you have from yourself.

If you live up to other people's expectations, you will never be truly happy.

Also... happiness is not something you look outside of yourself... but within you. If you expect that other people can make you happy, you are wrong.

Just think – what if they would leave tomorrow?

Yes, people can bring you joy, they can make you feel better about yourself... but that's usually just an instant feeling and something temporary.

30

"You don't need to be pretty like her. You can be pretty like you."

To all women and men: Do not compare yourself to others.

Please.

We are all, each and every one, unique in the whole Universe, and that's the beauty of life.

We are all beautiful, because we are different. There is no such thing as the most beautiful beauty! There is no such thing as perfection.

We were not born to compare ourselves to others... so, try to stay out of trends that make us look and behave the same.

Take care of yourself inside and outside.

Work on yourself to be better person in all aspects.

Look for progress, not perfection, so you could only compare yourself with who you were yesterday.

That's the only person you should compare yourself with, the one you look in a mirror every day.

I also like to say: they laugh at me because I'm different, I laugh at them because they are all the same.

I'm aware of the fact that I'm different. And I love it.

Accept and embrace your body and be gentle and kind to yourself.

31

"Don't try to change anyone, change how you deal with them."

You should accept people as they are.

Encourage them to be better persons BY BEING AN EXAMPLE, not by simply giving them your opinions & telling them to act in a certain way just because you think they should (No matter the good intentions).

If they want to change, they will, if not... they won't (ha-ha, a very intelligent sentence).

But that's true... simply accept them and focus on yourself... maybe you are the one who needs some change? For an instance in the way you look at them.

In case you find yourself spending time with someone who is causing you frustration or negative sensation, again, be aware that you can't change them. Instead, try to change how you deal with them (focusing on yourself and keeping your inner peace. Not easy, I know, but that's the only way to stay sane. Trust me, I know what I'm talking about, well, as usual).

32

"Stop looking for a partner. Focus on your goals and rebuilding your life. The right person will eventually find their way to you."

If you are single, the best thing you can do is to focus on yourself, to build your "kingdom", to enjoy your time, to learn how to be your best friend. The right one will show up. Eventually.

If that person doesn't show up, well, just think about all those people who are in relationships wishing to be single. So many of them.

I'm joking a bit (or not). The thing is, don't rush anything, instead of looking for the right person, work on being that right person.

33

"Nobody is too busy, it's just a matter of priorities."

The golden rule: Don't prioritize someone who treats you like an option!

We all find our time for things and people who matter to us. No excuses needed.

Therefore...

Invest smart... because it's your life! Your time. And time is the most precious gift you can give to someone. Time is the most valuable thing. So, make sure you don't waste it, because time won't come back. Be mindful of how, where and with whom you spend your time.

Don't prioritise people who treat you like an option or talk to you only in their free time or just when they need you.

Don't surround yourself with people who will drag you down, but with those who will lift you up.

Invest in yourself and people who appreciate your existence. Surround yourself with people with the same vision as yours, with likeminded people.

Talk with people who find the time to talk to you. To check how you are because they care.

Your time is precious. So is your energy.

And... don't get surprised if someone decides not to prioritise you. You will find the reasons in the stories above... what you give is what you get.

34

"As you leave the crowd in hot pursuit of a rare-air life, you will be misunderstood. Our world was built by people who the masses called 'weird'."

People will call you crazy just because they don't understand you.

This shouldn't stop you from trying and pursuing your dreams!

We all have a dream that we want to achieve. Believe in yourself!

Don't let anyone tell you that you can't do it! You can do It!

35

"Stop holding onto people just because you have history together!"

Let go of anything that is holding you back... whether we talk about friends, partners... you name it.

We usually tend to think that a true measurement of a good friendship is the years spent together behind us. The same goes for any kind of relationship.

So sometimes we linger on just because of that.

That can be quite wrong.

Unless you are lucky enough that both of you change in the same direction.

It makes no sense to stay friends/partners just because you have history together.

We change. We grow. Our interests can change as we grow and vary from one person to another. It is completely natural to let go of anyone or anything that is holding you back.

So always ask yourself what is the true reason you are holding on to someone?

36

"Acceptance from yourself is far more important than acceptance from others."

Read this again.

Don't look at yourself through the eyes of others!

Focus on yourself, connect with yourself, accept and embrace yourself, work on yourself. And others? Who cares what others think? Who cares whether they will accept you or not? Why that even matters?

You do you, as long as you do good to yourself and to others. And you will attract your tribe who will accept you for who you are and not for some false image you have created.

Yeah, we live in a world of people with false images they have created based on expectations others have from them. Simply because they believe they have to be accepted by others. To me, it sounds like you need the approval of your existence from others. That's just sad.

Mostly, people do it unconsciously. Because we've been taught to live that way. But knowing this now, you can change it. And if you keep continue to live like that, you decided it consciously.

Therefore, if you decide to live one UNhappy life then think what others think of You, how they see you and put the key of your happiness in their pocket.

You decide.

37

"How do you run away from things that are in your head?"

You can run, but you can't hide. Everything is still there, because you're running away from things that are in your head.

Thus, there is no point in running away.

You need to confront things you're running away from, by accepting them and looking for a solution.

Ignoring, running away, looking for remedies that will only give you an instant relief, these are all just temporary things.

Meanwhile, your problem is still there. A solution, look for a solution.

38

"It's in the eyes, always the eyes."

The power of eye contact! It's so important to look directly in the eyes of someone... for so many reasons.

- Eyes are the window to our soul

- Eye-to-eye contact is a powerful tool of communication

- You show your interest

- You show your respect

- You show your appreciation

- You can't hide emotions

- You show your understanding

And so on...

You can even fall in love like that. Eye contact is a powerful stimulator of love and affection.

39

"Someone can be madly in love with you and still not be ready. They can love you in a way you have never been loved and still not join you on the bridge. And whatever their reasons you must leave. Because you never ever have to inspire anyone to meet you on the bridge. You never ever have to convince someone to do the work to be ready. There is more extraordinary love, more love that you have never seen, out here in this wide and wild universe. And there is the love that will be ready." – Nayyirah Waheed

Again, beautifully said and explained!

Do not push anyone or anything, especially not those who aren't ready!

You might think that person is ready, just because you wish so... you might think that he/she is your perfect match, so you will try to convince and encourage that person to see the things you can see and you might be right, maybe they seem perfect for you, but, that's only in your head!

The truth is the person who is ready doesn't have to be convinced... That person will be available, willing and ready to commit.

Those who are ready – you will simply feel it.

You deserve love, the love you don't have to push! If you have to push it, leave. They first need to do their homework, and you can't force people to do that.

And please think over: Are you choosing someone who isn't

choosing you?

40

"Breaking up is the most difficult thing. It's never easy to start over. but it is better to feel the pain a day or two rather than being with someone and getting heartaches every single day. Love yourself enough to walk away from anything that makes you sad."

Breaking up is probably not the most difficult thing, but it is definitely very difficult. For so many reasons.

And maybe you will feel the pain for more than a day or two... but haven't you already suffered the pain being in a relationship without love? So...

41

"Until the lions have their own historians, the history of the hunt will glorify the hunter"- Chinua Achebe

History is written by the survivors/winners. Dead man can't write. Lions needs to learn how to write.

So, history... Have we learnt the truth from history?

As long as history will be written by hunters, lions will never be glorified.

Even everyday stories you hear, think twice before you believe it. After all, you have heard only one side of the story...

42

"What consumes your mind controls your life"

Everything starts with your thoughts. Bad thoughts actually manifest into bad things in real life. It's true.

Your mind is a very powerful tool. Rule your mind or let your mind rule you.

Choose your thoughts wisely! Thoughts that serve you, not destroy you.

43

"At your absolute best, you still won't be good enough for the wrong person. At your worst, you'll still be worth it to the right person." - Karen Salmansohn

The thing is, there are no wrong or right persons in relationships. There are those who are right or wrong FOR YOU. If someone is wrong for you, it doesn't mean that he/she is wrong for someone else.

If you didn't have couple of them who were "wrong" for you, how would you know who is right one for you? Maybe they were not wrong, maybe there were right at that point, something we actually needed? A lesson that we had to learn, so we don't attach to the same type of partners in our lives again.

Or maybe you were just lucky enough to find that perfect one without having to learn this.

Who knows. You know it better.

The thing is to find the perfect one, the one who is perfect FOR YOU. You define what that is. A weirdo who is compatible with your own weirdness.

Namaste.

44

"You either get bitter or you get better. It's that simple. You either take what has been dealt to you and allow it to make you a better person, or you allow it to tear you down. The choice does not belong to fate, it belongs to you." - Josh Shipp

The choice is yours!

Just think about this in case you start blaming everything or everyone else or start thinking how life isn't fair. No shit? And what about others who have willingly decided to get better?

You say life isn't fair to you? Really? Comparing to what? What if you are just one ungrateful person who doesn't appreciate the life you've been given? How about that?

Take responsibility for your decisions and grow up.

If you decide to get bitter just don't go around complaining, instead DO something to change your attitude. Change the mindset. The first step is to be aware of it. Consciousness, oh consciousness.

45

"In order to be in a happy relationship, you have to talk about the things that bother you... even if you agree to disagree."

You have to face any challenge! I mean you don't have to, it's your decision.

And we all have fears and doubts... but you gotta do what's right! We usually know when something is wrong, when something doesn't feel right, or simply when we don't like something. Yet, very often we refuse to speak about it. Instead, we ignore it, most of time because we fear other people's reactions... and that's not right! It's easy, but not the right thing to do!

You gotta face your fears. Most of the people don't do that.

Why?! Because it is a hard work... so it's much easier to ignore it.

People fear facing their fears. By choosing to ignore your fears, things can only get worse, because you suppress your emotions and what happens next? You become unhappy. You start to blame everything and everyone else but yourself. It starts to reflect on your life and people around you. Your relationship becomes unhealthy, just because you have decided to ignore and not face your "challenge" (whatever situation you might be in).

Good communication is a base for any healthy relationship. If you fear people's reactions 'cause they'll judge you, just think – how do you even know that will happen, maybe they won't judge you at all. If they do, you know what, then they shouldn't be in your life, therefore, why fearing them?

46

"Be the person you want to have in your life."

Usually people tend to expect a lot, yet only very few of them ask themselves how much they give.

You know what, you fucking deserve the love you give.

Exactly the same amount. And not just love, but any other thing in life as well.

So, if your love is immense... you deserve love immensely.

If you are loyal, you deserve loyalty.

Thus, if you are not loyal, no, I'm not wishing you to be with someone who is unfaithful, you are wishing that to yourself.

Like I said, you deserve reciprocity. You deserve everything you give. And what that would be, it depends on YOU.

Self-analysis.

Be silly. be fun. be different. be you. because life is too short to be anything but happy. enjoy every moment.

47

"You don't always need a logical reason for doing everything in your life. Do it because you want to; because it's fun; because it makes you happy."

Very true!

Enjoy your life, that's the point. Do what makes you happy. Don't care what others will think or what "advice" they will give you for the choices you make. Just listen to your heart. No one knows what's good for you better than you.

48

"Your elevation may require your isolation"

Oh, it does.

You will learn a lot about yourself like that.

You will learn how to become your best friend. You will discover new things about yourself, what you like or don't like… what inspires you. Your mind will become clearer, and you will start to pay attention to your thoughts.

Not just to your thoughts but so many other very important things… your surroundings, how you spend your time and with whom you spend it, what sucks your energy, what gives you energy…

But most importantly, spending time alone will lead you to self-love. And self-love is the most important thing, because among other things, you will learn how to stay true to yourself and how to live your life up to your expectations.

Staying true to yourself will bring you those who truly love you for who you are, not for some image you've created to look good in other people's eyes. So, please... spend some time alone.

After you realise how important it is to be alone, you will start craving those solitary moments when you can reconnect with yourself, pursuing your inner peace.

In solitude, one finds real strength. Make sure that the people you surround yourself with are building you up, NOT breaking you down. Reevaluate your relationships.

49

"Stop watering dead plants."

You gotta stop watering dead plants. Stop wasting your time and energy on things, people, relationships or anything that doesn't make you feel happy.

You (both) deserve happiness which equals fulfilment in your life.

50

"Don't use social media to impress people. Use it to impact people." - Dave Willis

Whether we talk about social media or life in general, whatever you do, do it for the right reasons. Do it because you have things to share, that will be beneficial for others. Do it because you can help others, do it because you have valuable things to say.

Again, it's all about intentions. Intentions speak of who we are. If you use social media to show off, so other can admire you and feed your ego, this speaks so much how superficial and unhappy you are. And those who admire your showing off are at the next level of unhappiness.

You know, I wish you all that life you post on Instagram or

Facebook is something you have FOR REAL. All day long. All year round. Try to impact and positively influence others. BE REAL.

Talk real… but most importantly, walk the talk.

51

"Go after dreams not people." - Paulo Coelho

Do not go after a guy, girl or anyone unless you think they deserve your attention.

Know the difference between chasing and conquering.

Don't even run after a bus, the next one will always come.

Pursue your dreams, not people!

52

"I told you so." Sincerely yours, Your intuition.

You know that feeling that comes from within telling you that something stinks? And you do it anyway?

Yeah, we have all been there, done that. Next time, try to listen to this feeling.

53

"We think too much and feel too little." - Charlie Chaplin

Try to listen to your heart… it will never lie to you.

Close your eyes and feel… whatever you do, your guidance should be Your heart.

Your brain serves for logical things, to guide you how to do something, to get you from point a to point b…

If you listen to your brain… it can lead you to overthinking, and that's something we want to avoid.

54

"Nothing is worth it if you aren't happy"

This should be your only scale to measure fulfilment of your life. Or happiness.

But first...

Define what happiness means to you.

Whether we talk about job, relationships, friendships, your hobbies, how you spend your time... name it... always ask yourself this: Does this makes me happy?

When you answer that question, you will know what to do.

55

"We are defined by our choices including the ones we never make."

All the choices you made today will define your tomorrow.

All the choices you didn't make today, will also define your tomorrow.

You are the creator of your life.

56

"Only those who care about you can hear you when you're quiet."

The quieter you become, the more you are able to hear and see... and learn!

Just sit down, observe and you might consider taking some

popcorns along the way.

People can react, let's say, very strangely and very differently when you become quiet. Even those who are close to you can really surprise you.

It happens, it happens...

57

"LIFE HACK: You literally don't have to be friends with people you don't like."

Why are you friends with someone you don't like?

Why do you say that you like someone if you don't?

Why do you spend your time with someone you don't like?

Why do you hang around with people who doesn't make you feel good about yourself?

Why do you stay in a relationship without love?

Why do you like posts you don't even read?

Ok, ok, the last one was just a test. Or not. But you know your why for any of these.

Bye

58

"Don't be afraid to give someone a compliment today."

Why aren't we afraid of judging others, insulting others etc.?

Yet we are afraid of giving genuine honest compliments?

In both cases, it's your ego talking.

I encourage you to give some random HONEST compliment when you see something nice in others. Today, tomorrow or every single day. Just watch their reaction after that. And pay attention on how you feel about it.

59

"So, do it. Decide. Is this the life you want to live? Is this the person you want to love? Is this the best you can be? Can you be stronger? Kinder? More compassionate? Decide. Breathe in. Breathe out and decide." - Meredith Grey

And act based on your decision! (The most important part)

Change what needs to be changed and try not to worry about those things you can't change. Things that simply don't depend on you. Worrying won't help.

Are you aware that we made tons of decision throughout the day?

Know that those decisions you made today create your life tomorrow. Be aware of it.

I like to say:

Practice, consistence, progression, not perfection.

60

"You are allowed to make mistakes."

That's how we learn, fail and grow!

We all make mistakes! It is FINE. But...

Know also that, if you repeat it more than once, it's no longer a mistake, but a choice!

Or just in case that you want and need to be sure that you have made a mistake, then repeat the same thing like 5 or 6 times until you learn a lesson. It happens, it happens...

61

"Be yourself. People don't have to like you, and you don't have to care."

Be a good person, always a better version of yourself.

Do good (whatever and whenever you can) for you and for the others.

People will judge you anyway. So why would you care about it? Why...

Not everyone will like you, neither should they.

Some people like green tea, some of them prefer black tea and some of them just like coffee. Got it?

62

"If you're good at something, never do it for free!"

The golden rule!

The "strange" thing is that other people think you should always do things for free once you have done something for them.

If you keep doing it, they will get used to it, and usually take it and you for granted.

We teach others how to treat us by what we allow them. This can be tricky, at least in my case. I always thought that it would be respected, the same way I showed respect. They would know their limits like I do. But that was my "mistake", 'cause we usually think that others think the same way we do. Once you set your limits and learn how to say no, oh boy, their reactions can, let's say, be amusing to observe. Even if I explain how I feel. They don't hear it, they just hear that NO. Like, how the fuck dare you say no to me?

So, you need to ask yourself a couple of questions, and answer them as well. Something like, do I need this in my life etc.?

63

"Some people create their own storms, then get upset when it rains."

We all know them.

So, when they get upset, they will start blaming everything/everyone else, anything but themselves.

Know that it has nothing to do with you.

Let them argue with themselves, so do yourself a favour and step back. For your own peace of mind.

And to all of those who point finger at others when it starts to rain: try this method – start pointing at yourself first. Take responsibility for your life.

You know, usually it's always the one with dirty hands who point fingers at others.

64

"Everyone wants a strong woman until she actually stands up, flexes her muscles and lets her voice out. Suddenly, she becomes *too much*. She has *forgotten where her place was*. People love those women as mere ideas, as fantasies. Not as breathing, living humans threatening to be even better than you could ever be."

Everyone wants a strong woman. It's a fact.

But…

The question is are you strong enough for her?

You see… Everyone wants her, but she doesn't need anyone. So, trust me if I say, if she chooses you, it's not because she needs you, but because she wants you. Not for your looks, but for your strength. For your values. Simply for being a man. Real man. Not a guy, but a MAN with integrity.

This is the answer about whether she is *too much* for you. It's about you.

65

"It's no use going back to yesterday, because I was a different person then." - Lewis Carroll

Learn from your past, but leave your past there, where it belongs. It doesn't exist anymore.

Decisions that you made yesterday, you live them today, so If you don't like your present, change something for the future.

Step by step. Small decisions and small changes are very important, they can lead you to some extraordinary things.

But the change starts with you.

66

"Once you feel avoided by someone never disturb them again."

If you have any self-respect and dignity kindly remove yourself from their lives.

If you don't understand the message behind "being avoided", try harder to understand that if someone is avoiding you, they are not interested in you.

This doesn't mean that you are not amazing. Just recognize the message between the lines from those who have no guts to tell you the truth, looking to your eyes.

And if they have told that to you kindly, then read the first sentence again and leave them alone.

67

"Be honest about your intentions with everything. You never want to build any type of relationship on lies. That foundation will always fail."

Our intentions speak about ourselves!

Whatever we do, before doing it we should ask ourselves why we want to do that or say that in the first place.

Oh, sometimes your answer can surprise you. Badly. All this can be improved, of course, but only if you are honest with yourself.

Do what's right, not what's easy! It's that simple.

68

"If only closed minds came with closed mouths."

There are two types of people in this world:

1 People who understand & appreciate sarcasm

2 Idiots.

(please don't take this seriously, if you did, read it again. Apart from that mind-mouth connection, in which case, I seriously mean it.)

69

"Why are we supposed to say it's okay when it's not?"

One of those questions I don't like been asked is: How are you?

No, there's nothing wrong with this question at all. If you really want to know how that person feels.

Unfortunately, among other words and questions we hear repeatedly, this one serves for almost anything, but for genuine interest about a person's wellbeing. And that's exactly what this question should mean: it should show you care.

Instead, it serves for starting a conversation, for approaching someone and so on and so forth.

Someone taught us that this question means we are being polite and kind.

Someone taught us that replying with *I'm ok* is being kind and polite.

You know, you shouldn't bother others with your problems. Thus, if you fall apart from within, and someone asks you how you feel, you should simply be polite, smile and reply: I'm ok.

How ridiculous.

This is so wrong. This is so fake! What makes you a polite and kind person is not a question, but your intention.

And if you want to start a conversation, please use your imagination and be more creative.

70

"Wow she really left our toxic relationship to be in a happy relationship?"

How dare you leave a toxic environment? How-dare-you?! How dare you wish one happy life fulfilled with love?

You should just stay there and accumulate that toxicity within your body and live up to other people's expectations. That's a perfect recipe for getting sick.

Don't you dare leave them, no, no. Don't think about yourself, your health and your personal fulfilment. Think about others and how to please them. That way you will not disappoint them, nor your family and all those that might judge you.

Change starts within you. The first step is to be conscious about what makes you feel good.

Please think about yourself. Because no one else will, unless you do...

71

"It's amazing how stupid you can be when you're in love..."

Naaah, you're not stupid!

Actually, you feel like you can move the mountains, there's nothing stupid about that.

People do crazy things when they're in love, yet again, there's nothing crazy about these things they make you feel like you have wings.

From a person-not-in-love's perspective, all these things seem crazy and stupid. But hey, that's all love, love doesn't know of logic.

72

"Never take your crown off to make weak-ass people feel comfortable."

Neva'! Being strong is something that life teaches us, putting us in all different types of situations. If we are willing to learn. How we deal with those situations will determine whether we will become strong(er) or weak(er).

It's up to every single one of us.

So, tell me again, why would you take your crown off so others could feel comfortable? If you've been through hell, and you kept walking like myself, tell me why would you allow others disrespect you?

And, in the first place, respect yourself! As well as others! But neva', NEVA' shrink yourself for the sake of others who refuse to grow.

73

"And the deeper you become, the more some don't know how to deal with it. Because the deeper you become, the more truth you reveal. And truth scares the hell out of some. Stay deep anyways." – J.M. Storm

And this is soooo true.

People usually fear things they don't know and again, that's the product of our thoughts. Judgments based on their level of self-consciousness.

They will call you crazy just because they don't understand you.

You should not shrink yourself so others could feel comfortable around you.

If they are not interested in learning and understanding, do yourself a favour, wish them all the best and let them go.

74

"When you love someone age, weight, height, distance, is just a number."

Your soul knows what's good for you!

Age is just a number. I know people in their 20s feeling like they are 50 years old and vice versa. Why should age difference be a problem? To whom and why? Who said that?

Immaturity is a problem and it has nothing to do with age.

If you love someone it's not for their looks, but for who they are and how they make you feel.

Distance? What's that if not a test to see is your love is real or not!

75

"Focus on where you want to go, not on what you fear." - Anthony Robbins

Your focus determines your reality.

So, your reality speaks for itself.

In case that some things don't depend on you... Let's say you're stuck somewhere you don't want to be, but you have to be there at the moment, for the time being.

Try not to focus on your current situation but repeat this: my current situation is not my final destination! (Tough struggles! I know, I know...)

In case that things depend on you, but you do nothing to change them, then you deserve them. Whether it is your fear stopping you, and usually it is, or any other thing... Don't blame life or others.

76

"If it's destroying you, then it isn't love, my dear."

My dear, LOVE HEALS.

Stop believing that love is something that hurts you, only people who doesn't know how to love can hurt you. Love never hurts. Learn the difference.

77

"Deep conversations with someone who understands you is everything."

It's like the best medicine you will ever get. And everything that your soul needs.

Yet we live in a very superficial world, so finding that one you can feel comfortable with, to open your soul, it's like a treasure.

Keepers.

But the most important thing is... be that one who understand. Be that keeper.

78

"Close some doors. Not because of pride, incapacity or arrogance, but simply because they no longer lead somewhere."
- Paulo Coelho

This is not selfish, but self-love.

This should be part of your self-care routine too.

Make sure that you are not guided by your ego. Listen to your body, and your soul, if it feels tired, that should be a sign.

For an instance if you repeatedly have to say the same exact thing about how you feel, if someone hurts you, if you want to fix things etc., and they repeatedly do the same exact thing over and over again, know that they don't respect you! You just get tired from that, emotionally and physically. And you will feel alone and lonely in the end. That's the sign, right?

I don't care, and neither should you whether they can't, won't or whatever... they simply don't. We all can if we want.

So, bye-bye. Don't touch my aura with your dirty hands.

And if you choose to close that door (maybe it won't be easy, but it will be necessary), another "advice" would be: don't open that door anymore, rather focus on... the window.

Seriously, focus on some new things that are waiting for you, things that will bring you joy!

79

"One morning she woke up different. Done with trying to figure out who was with her, against her, or walking down the middle because they didn't have the guts to pick a side. She was done with anything that didn't bring her peace. She realized that opinions were a dime a dozen, validation was for parking, and loyalty wasn't a word, but a lifestyle. It was this day that her life changed. And not because of a man or a job but because she realized that life is way too short to leave the key to your happiness in someone else's pocket. It was the day life began!"

No, she didn't wake up different.

Things don't happen overnight. I wish they did. I know lots of people wish that things just change without putting any effort to it, 'cause *it's going to hurt*. But I must disappoint you guys, life doesn't work that way.

It is a fucking hard work, dealing with situations and confronting them.

Face to face. And what I know, what I learned by now is that I know nothing. Life is a journey and our teacher and we learn through our experiences. Therefore, we change all the time.

The only thing that might happen overnight and that can make you wake up different is some dream that made you realize you need some change.

Decide and act.

80

"Your bad days don't define you. Take a few breaths, let today go, and focus your energy on the future." - Billy Chapata.

The same way, your good days don't define you.

A curious thing is that people give too much importance to those bad days and when everything goes smoothly, they accept is as a kind of a normal thing...

Good days, less good days... that's all life. And your life doesn't define you.

YOU DEFINE YOUR LIFE!

"You can go to the moon and back for someone and they'll have the audacity to say: I never asked you to, tho'."

Oh, for sure lots of people will instantly think: oh, I would love that someone goes to the moon and back for me (duuuh, of course we all want that), otherwise they are ungrateful, selfish etc.

(Just another perspective) But are they really selfish? No! The person who went to the moon and back is the selfish one!

I know I know, pfff, mind blowing...

In case that someone was honest by saying that that's not the love that they need, want, dream of... then they were completely honest & in alignment with them and with you. Respect that. Don't push just because you want them, believing they are perfect for you. The question is why would you go to the moon & back if they don't want that?

Thus, the person who expects to be loved just because they would do anything for someone, is selfish and that can be very exhausting.

Don't push the things if they don't flow naturally, feel other person's needs and expect from that other person to listen to your needs.

If you match, perfect, if you don't match... perfect again, wish all the best to each other and say bye-bye.

You know, sometimes, even with our best intention for others, we can do things that simply are not good for them!

So before you go to the moon, make sure you know where are you heading to, otherwise don't come back at all.

82

"I don't have an attitude problem. You have a problem with my attitude and that's not my problem."

Why some (most) people tend to think that you get angry if you distance yourself for whatever reasons. (People who distance themselves without getting angry – yes, we do exist, I promise.)

Or that you are aggressive if your opinion is different than theirs and you say it openly to their face? You know, they think they have the right to have an opinion about things, but when you express your own, they just don't like it if that opinion is different than their own.

Or if they make you feel uncomfortable with their words (or jokes) and you express your discomfort? Instead of understanding you they get offended because you didn't like it? Sooo ridiculous.

And so on...

All of these have one thing in common. Their ego speaks so loudly, their insecurities, frustrations, immaturity are so loud they can't hear anything but themselves.

People who don't know how to communicate will always say that you like to argue!

Don't try to convince them or explain yourself if you see that they can't hear you. Try to keep your inner peace, and let them go.

But, the most important thing is: don't be that one who is driven by their own ego.

83

"Two things define you: Your patience when you have nothing and your attitude when you have everything." - George Bernard Shaw

Among other things, this definitely speaks about yourself.

Those moments, decisions you make define you.

For instance, when you have everything, let's say some kind of power, when your job position is "superior" than jobs of your co-workers.

You can always choose how you will treat them. If you treat them inferiorly using your power, that's some big issue within you.

I always picture who hides behind that behaviour. Some kid who was bullied in school and didn't heal its wounds? Problems at home?

Whatever might be the reason, understand that sharing your frustrations using your power won't make you feel good about yourself in a long run. It might give you some food for your ego, but that's just temporary. Over the time, you will only feel worse.

And the most important thing is that it doesn't make you a good person. At all.

84

"Politeness has become so rare that some people mistake it for flirtation."

Kindness, politeness and having manners have become so rare nowadays that people mistake them for flirting.

Don't mix these two. I'm kind to everyone at first. You're not special to me because of that. It's not about you, but me and my upbringing.

Also, people mix being kind with being weak.

Again, the way you see others speaks about yourself!

Self-care is not selfish. self-care is a priority and necessity.

85

"They always come back especially when you've moved on…"

Of course, they do! Always…

Why?

If you are a free spirit and if you know how to love, they will always come back.

The reason why they come back is not because of you, I must say, but because they know where they have been loved in the right way. They know where they've felt good in their own skin.

I wish that they come back because they finally started to love themselves, but usually that's not the case.

86

"Love is not what you say. Love is what you do."

Love is an action!

You just can't sit down and feel love for someone waiting to be loved in return 'cause, you know, you looooove that someone so much so they should love you back just because of that. I mean, you can try…

Also, don't promise something you are not capable of doing. Don't play with other people's emotions if you are not secure in your own. Don't awake other people's feelings without feeling the same and without any genuine intention of loving that person.

Oh, the intentions are soooo important, our intentions speak about ourselves. Not purely actions, but intentions behind them as well!

It's that simple!

87

"Self-care is not selfish."

Self-care is even MORE important:

- addressing your "problematic" thoughts, fears, even your behaviour (like the consequences of stress and frustrations that has been built up within)

- removing toxic people

- replacing old habits that no longer serve you for the new ones that brings you joy

- being in harmony with your thoughts - your words - your actions

- being responsible for what you say and do

- being responsible for your life, working on yourself

And so on...

Everything comes from within.

So, if you try to fix your problems, remember that everything goes from the inside out, and not vice versa.

You can put masks on your face, you can do surgeries you can do whatever you want and it will only help you feel better for a day or two for a week or a month. And that's nice, but if you truly want to take care of yourself, then dig deep.

And... Fix the problem, not the consequences.

Because self-care is not selfish, it's self-love!

88

"How to explain when you have a very messy and chaotic mind."

When you feel like this, and we all have experienced this... don't even try to figure out what's going on there, just go back to bed and wait for the next day.

I'm joking, but seriously, don't try to explain that feeling, because it's impossible to see the clear picture when you are upset. Instead, focus on calming yourself down, doing things that will bring you peace. When you clear your mind, the answer will show up even without too much thinking.

89

"These pains you feel are messengers. Listen to them." – Rumi

Don't make a common mistake in the times of suffering, trying to forget about the pain. Or ignore it.

When you feel the pain, it's usually a sign that something is not right. For instance, if someone hurts you, instead of blaming them, try to ask yourself why that happened? What is that pain telling you? Do you need to learn something from it?

Only with an attitude of accepting, encountering and under-standing can we become aware of anything.

90

"The person who says it cannot be done should not interrupt the person doing it." -Chinese Proverb

They shouldn't, but they usually do. Usually because they think they can't do something or they wish, but they don't do anything about it. So, if you pursue your dreams they will interrupt you. Why? Because they won't feel happy if you succeed... God forbid, if you succeed.

Don't let them interrupt you If you think you can, then yes, you CAN. Just do it, don't let anyone tell you what you can and can't do or achieve, even if you chase the moon, because who knows, you just might catch it.

Seriously, if you want to achieve anything, do something about it, go and get it! Don't pay attention to every dog that barks on you. It will only distract you from pursuing your dreams.

91

"It's okay to live a life others don't understand." - Jenna Woginrich

Please follow your inner voice, follow your dreams. Let your heart guides you.

It's your life, make sure to live it up to your expectations.

You shouldn't let other people's opinions about your life affect you at all. If they don't understand, so what? The most important thing is that you understand it.

92

"Sometimes, you have to pretend that you're happy and fine."

I strongly disagree!

I strongly believe that one should always talk about how they feel. If things are not ok and you don't feel ok you should talk about it with your dear ones. Of course, talk in order to find a solution, don't talk to complain. Or just to feel easier by taking out all that bothers you. This makes a huge difference.

Say NO to suppressing your feelings, NO to pretending that you're ok, NO, NO, NO. I know that we all struggle from time to time, sometimes very often, yet people don't speak about it mostly 'cause they fear the judgment. Know that you're not alone! You would be surprised to know how many people feel the same as you do.

Don't believe everything you read on internet, look for what is reasonable to you.

93

"Nothing kills you like your mind"

Worrying, overthinking, fears, doubts, creating non-existing scenarios. Sound familiar?

You can either be your best friend or your worst nightmare.

Learn how to observe your thoughts and how to rule your mind! Your mind is a very powerful tool.

We all think 24/7 - be kind to yourself and choose thoughts that will serve you!

94

"She is what the world loves to hate – pure, authentic, tested, and brave. And that is why her kind will save this world."
- Johnny Nguyen

Thought of the day, week, year.

Being your true self, having a free spirit and living according to your values and expectations is a rare thing to see today.

Most people, consciously or not, live up to other people's expectations (This is something that even freest of spirits can struggle with, but at least they acknowledge it).

That's why people will hate you. Not because of you, but because they wish to live that way, but they don't. Not because they can't, of course they can, but they just don't.

The same goes for others who will love everything about you, they'll admire the things you do, how you act, they will feel great in your company. Because that's what free spirits do, they don't judge you, they will make you feel comfortable in your own skin.

I don't mind being loved or hated. Or judged. I don't think that way. I don't think about those who love me or not, that's not in my focus. If I have a positive influence in the world and make a positive impact on others, that's the only thing that matters to me.

Namaste.

95

"You learn a lot about people when they don't get what they want."

Haha, oh, yes!

Then you see their real intentions! You see their true selves.

For an instance, when someone approaches you, (virtually or not, either way) with sweet, kind, sugar coated words, and you don't want to talk to them (for whatever reasons, that's your right) they usually get offended and all that sweetness melts away in no time. Or they simply disappear. They can even block you (don't ask me how I know this).

Obviously, their intention was hidden behind these sweet words. Once they didn't get what they wanted, their ego stepped out.

If you ask me, they are fake, insecure people. And for what it matters, I don't even like fake nails.

96

"What would you do if you weren't afraid?"

Know that your fears and worries are the product of your thoughts! Thus, the only person who is stopping you from doing things is you!

Everything is 'figureoutable', maybe not easy, BUT POSSIBLE!

97

"You will be too much for some people. Those aren't your people." - Glennon Doyle

I've heard this too many times. Using those exact words or phrases like *too deep, too honest* etc.

I'm not sure whether these people are aware that when they say something like that, they automatically say about themselves they are "too shallow", "too little ", "not honest"...

I think they are not aware what their statements imply. At least I hope so.

Either way, none of my business. Those are certainly not my people.

98

"Helping one person might not change the whole world, but it could change the world for one person."

Please, never ask someone how they are doing unless your intention is to really know how they are doing. If it is, then prepare to truly listen to them.

Listen to that person. Sometimes, that can be enough to help (In case they are not doing well). If you see that you can help even more, do it.

The world needs more love and more healers.

You will not save the world, but maybe you will change their world for the better. Imagine that impact you can have on someone's life!!!

Disclaimer: this is not for those victims who look for "help". These people are just looking for someone's attention so they can drain them by blaming everything and everyone else but themselves. Those need other type of help.

99

"The biggest coward of a man is to awaken the love of a woman without the intention of loving her." - Bob Marley

"Only cowards hide behind silence" – Paulo Coelho

Another thing I can't stress enough is that our intentions (whatever we do on daily basis) ultimately speak about ourselves. We should be asking ourselves before we do something: why do we do It, what's our intention with it.

Oh, this will tell you so much about yourself.

So, if you awake woman's love and her feelings without intentions of loving her, it speaks about yourself alone and how cowardly you act (among other things).

The worst thing you can do is to let her think that everything is ok, while you know it's not! What usually happens is that you disappear without saying a word! Or without giving her a proper explanation.

Coward times 2

Be mature enough to speak openly if something goes wrong, or if you lose your interest for whatever reason. Do not let her think, the same way you wouldn't like to be left thinking about it.

As Mahatma Gandhi said: "A coward is incapable of exhibiting love; it is the prerogative of the brave."

Grow some guts instead of growing a fake image to gain some attention.

Of course, it goes the same the other way around as well.

100

"I don't like forced conversations, forced friendships, forced interactions. I simply do not force things. If we do not vibe, we don't vibe."

If you feel that I am hard to get along with you, let's say that's probably because I just don't want to get along with you. Simply 'cause the people you spend time with influence your attitudes, thoughts and your successfulness. I really, REALLY don't want negative people in my life. Ignore, remove, block. Easy peasy.

101

"When you can tell your story and it doesn't make you cry, that's when you know you've healed." – David Wolfe

This is soooo true... That's the measurement of knowing if you have gotten over something/someone or not.

If it still hurts when you talk or think about It, it means – it's not healed.

If you can talk about it without a lump in your throat, that means you are (on the good way) to overcome it. Or you have already healed.

And if you haven't healed, just remember: every time you think about that specific situation that hurt you, your body produces exactly the same chemicals as when it happened. So, you're putting yourself through the same stress. Over and over again, you're feeling the same pain. And you will keep doing it until you decide to work on how to let it go.

The importance of acceptance, forgiveness and letting go of situations or people that have wronged or hurt us is crucial.

Acceptance doesn't mean approval.

Give yourself some time, but do work on that. Time heals nothing, you need to work on it and learn how to live with it. And for that you need time. Your time.

Everything you do, you're doing it because you need that inner peace.

102

"Oh, no. No, I'm not okay. I just decided being sad is a waste of time." – Jackie from *That '70s Show*

What If?

What if you choose not to stress over life and situations in life.

It is is quite challenging but also important to understand that you do not have control over life, but what you do have control over is how you will react.

103

"The 5 x 5 Rule: If it's not gonna matter in 5 years, don't spend more than 5 minutes being upset by it."

If you worry about something, just ask yourself: will worrying about it help you?

If the answer is yes, then keep worrying and I will give you all my problems to worry about them too.

Seek for a solution instead of worrying. If you worry too much, your mind won't be clear and you won't be able to see a solution. Instead, it will give you a chronic headache.

So why worry?

104

"If you are not doing what you love, you are wasting your time." - Billy Joel

If you are with someone you don't love,

if you don't love your workouts (no matter their type),

if you don't spend your free time the way you would love to,

if you don't like your job,

if you eat food you don't like,

you are wasting your time.

The good news is that you are in charge of all this, and you can change it.

Always.

It's never too late to start over.

105

"I set my boundaries to respect myself, not to offend you"

I can't stress enough the importance of knowing your limits and setting boundaries. That is so important! When you learn how to love and respect yourself, setting limits will come as a "consequence". You can't please everybody, and if you try to do it, you might as well lose yourself.

People should know their limits in any kind of relationships. Usually, they don't. This includes maintaining good communication, emotional intelligence, empathy, education. Well, to me, all this is a part of good communication.

Setting boundaries means knowing what you can give and share with whom, without getting drained. But also, it defines what you need from those relationships.

Yet, people get offended by that. How's that? That's ridiculous. But it's none of your business. If you gave everything you could give, and they get offended because you didn't give what they wanted, stay away from them. Let them grow up. It's all about expectations here. People tend to expect so much more than they give.

Another excellent quote: "I'll not let anyone walk through my mind with their dirty feet" - Gandhi

Step back, don't touch my aura with your dirty hands, this is my space. - myself.

106

"Apparently, when you treat people the same way they treat you, they get offended."

Don't you dare treat them like they treat you... Don't you dare. They are allowed to upset you to, piss you off, disrespect you, be rude... but don't you dare do them the same.

It's ironic, right?

But at the end of the day, try not to be affected by those whose intentions are not good when it comes to you, rise above them and step back. You don't need any unnecessary drama in your life. You don't need drama at all. And especially not drama queens.

Why? Because our actions speak about ourselves... It's nothing personal, and sooner or later, these people will start focusing on someone else instead.

107

"Every good thing that has happened in your life happened because something changed." -Andy Andrews.

Ok?

Change is usually a good thing. So, don't fear the change. Your fears are nothing but your thoughts and that's your mind telling you to stay in your comfort zone.

Remember that change starts with you. Everything great that

has ever happened has begun as a single thought in someone's mind. We are all capable of thinking, right? What stops you then?

108

"You can't force chemistry to exist where it doesn't in the same way you can't deny it when it does."

You simply shouldn't deny how you feel. You can't force things to happen just because you wish so. Neither of these two has led to anything good. Always express how you feel and let go of anything that doesn't flow.

109

"Above all don't ever change just to impress who says you're not good enough. Change because it makes you a better person and leads you to a brighter future."

Above all, if you change yourself to impress others, they will like the image of you, not your true self. And that can become a real problem later...

We can witness this on daily basis, people try to impress each other instead of focusing on themselves and who they are... Don't allow anyone to make you feel like you're not good enough. There is no need to pretend to be someone you're not.

Be yourself and the right people will love you. Because the people worth impressing just want you to be yourself.

110

"If everybody likes you, you have a serious problem."

It's impossible to make everyone like you. Don't even try. And if you do, read the first sentence again.

You're probably doing something wrong.

If you think that everyone likes you or you still try to please everybody, you have a serious problem.

111

"I'm going to give you the same amount of effort as you give me."

Wow... I saw this and booom! Such a great quote for self-analysis.

People usually "want" something but they don't put enough

effort to achieve that.

Yet, they love being a priority in other people's lives.

They love when they get attention and usually get used to it quickly. In the end, they take it for granted, so as that person.

No matter the type of relationship, the romantic or the friendly one, if you want to be close with someone, ask yourself what would be if you received the same amount of effort as you gave? What would it be then? Think before it's too late... So, if someone decide to leave you, ask yourself about your amount of effort involved.

Effort reflects interest. You can't always expect to receive, one needs to give in order to receive.

If you are a giver and always put an effort, don't let that exhaust you, know your limits, simply ask yourself this:

Am I receiving the same amount of effort as I'm giving?

112

"There's nothing wrong with asking for help."

Don't ever feel ashamed to ask for help!

Not that there's nothing to fear. Asking for help requires some guts.

Admitting you need help is a sign of strength, not weakness.

113

"Sometimes holding on does more damage than letting go."

You literally make a damage to YOUR BODY, YOUR HEALTH when

you hold on something that doesn't make you feel good. Name it: people, relationships, situations in life, emotions, just NAME it!

Let go of anything that doesn't make you feel good! It's not easy, but as you can see, it's so important!

Your health is the most important thing, it should be number 1 on your priority list.

114

"Stay away from people who can't take responsibility for their actions and who make you feel bad for being angry at them when they do you wrong."

A must.

If you want to stay out of drama.

But, first of all, I hope you are responsible for your actions as well (especially towards others). If you are, stay away from those who aren't.

Don't fight with them, 'cause you won't win and it's a complete waste of your time and your energy. You won't convince them that they are wrong. That's something they need to learn and to acknowledge themselves.

And you...

Try to keep your inner peace and surround yourself with people similar to you.

115

"Love is not what you say, it's what you do."

Dont be just blah blah blah. Mean what you say and do what

you preach! The world is full of blah blah blah people, but your action will reveal you. And then you will lose your value and credibility, and then what?

Don't play with other people's emotions, especially if you're unsure of your own.

Oooor, even worse, don't play with someone's heart if you have no serious intentions. It's a sign of weakness and immaturity.

116

"If you're helping someone and expecting something in return, you are doing business, not kindness" - Gurbaksh Chahal

Be kind. Always.

Think about your intention when you want to "help" someone. Your intention will tell you a lot about yourself.

Ask yourself: Is that how you would like to be helped?

And to go back to the quote: Do not confuse help with business!

117

"If it gets awkward, let it be awkward. That awkwardness is something they created. You don't owe anyone a performance of being okay when you are not feeling okay so that they can feel better about themselves." - Jennifer Peepas

Don't be people-pleaser so they can feel better about themselves, if you feel that you can't give yourself fully. Know your limits.

If you don't feel good, simply please yourself with some TLC (Tender Loving Care).

If you are afraid to show that you are not feeling well, because you think they will look at you in a different way, that's wrong!

Allow yourself to BE! To feel and accept all emotions you experience. So, if you don't feel well, go through it without suppressing feelings, 'cause you should be your priority.

And you deserve people who will understand that, not those who will upset you even more because you don't give them daily portion of what-ever-they-expect from you. You are not in a circus for the sake of cookies!

118

"6 + 3 = 9 but so does 5 + 4. The way you do things isn't always the only way to do them. Respect other people's way of thinking."

We all see the same thing, but we speak from very different perspectives.

Our perspectives can vary and depend on so many things: education, experience, beliefs, etc. So, we don't see the things as they are, but through who we are.

In order to have one decent respectful conversation, we should strive to avoid misunderstandings by simply expressing our perspectives over the same thing. Be sure that you both express what that thing means to You. Your definition. Your perspective. That's the start of one good conversation.

If you talk about love, speak of your definition of love. Then listen what other person says about love. You would be surprised how people see the same thing in a very different way.

Try to respect other people's point of view rather than to be right. Respect other people's way of thinking the same way you would like to be respected.

It's that simple.

119

"If you expect something in return for being a nice person, you aren't a nice person."

You know definitions in life are so important. Why? To avoid any confusion, misunderstandings and simply things should be called by their proper name.

For example:

If you express your love to someone you love, expecting nothing in return is unconditional love. If you expect something, that's not pure love but conditional love.

If you help someone expecting nothing, that's kindness and help with pure heart. If you expect something in return, that's not help, that's business.

If you are nice to all, you are simply one nice genuine person, if you are nice to one person and not to others you are not nice, you are just looking for some benefit.

And soooooo on. You see it's quite simple. People confuse these things and that's what makes this life complicated. Be honest with yourself first.

120

"Never underestimate the power of good morning texts, apologies, and random compliments."

Truuuuue... I really love waking up seeing morning messages from people I love, as well as good night texts. It is all about little things that make you feel loved and happy! It is nice to know and to have people who really care about you, so never take them for granted!

I enjoy giving random compliments even to strangers, I love to see them smiling!

121

"Your wound is probably not your fault but healing is your responsibility" - Denice Frohman

If you don't take responsibility for your life, no one will do that for you! You are in charge of how you feel, so if you can't control life, you can control your reactions to everything that happens to you. I don't mean that you are not allowed to feel sad, to cry, to feel disappointed, quite the opposite. I encourage you to feel every emotion, but also to be your own hero.

122

"As you start to walk on the way, the way appears." - Rumi

The first step is the hardest one.

People fear way too many things, they don't even dare to make that first step. And they get stuck.

And again, it's all in your head. You're the only one stopping you from making that first step.

It can be anything you think about. Starting your business, getting divorced, asking someone out, saying that you're sorry, travelling, saying I love you, literally ANYTHING.

Fear is not real. Fear is a product of our thoughts. Thoughts are generated based on past experience, beliefs, teachings and so on.

The most common fear is the fear of failure (in anything). So, you decide to stay in your safe zone. It's easier. At least, it seems like a safe zone. You think it's better not to risk, because what if... now, I'll let you continue this sentence yourself.

As you can see, those are nothing but your thoughts and you letting your fears guide you and make you act based on your fears.

And what if you succeeded? Would you make that first step?

We all get lost, but keep in mind that a way out ALWAYS appears, as long as you make that first step.

123

"Don't ever mistake my silence for ignorance, my calmness for acceptance or my kindness for weakness. Compassion and tolerance are not a sign of weakness, but a sign of strength." - Dalai Lama

Something I've experienced way too many times, and I still do.

Usually, you can learn a lot about people through the way they treat you — it speaks a lot about themselves.

So, what I'm learning to do in these cases — I just step away. I don't need that kind of people in my life. At all! I'm learning to let go of anything or anyone that mistake my personality with their image of me.

Ciao, ciao... 'cause this is my space, step away & don't touch my aura with your dirty hands.

124

"Would you marry my needs?"

You know we live in the world of superficial values…

People try to impress each other with material things & physical appearance, and that is ok, as long as you feel happy and fulfilled. If that is your limit then OK! Just don't complain how nobody can see "true you".

Me, I love beautiful minds and soul. I love people with integrity. With strength and good manners. Who can show you a different world, from their own perspective, so I can learn something new, maybe something I actually love and didn't have a clue about. People who know to treat you right, with whom you can speak about everything. Of course, this has to be vice versa as well. Like everything in life.

Don't get me wrong, of course I love nice stuff, BUT that's not something I'm looking for. That's not the way you can impress me. I don't accept this superficial world as a part of my life. Yes, sometimes it can be really difficult, because people think the better restaurant they invite you, the better car they drive you in, the more will they impress you. They will "have you" with it. In the end, to me it all looks very sad. Is that everything you have to show? Good, you happy, me happy, but not with you.

125

"Everyone is so caught up with toning and shaping their ass that they forget to tone and shape their character."

If you're pretty, you're pretty. That's nothing but: Congratulations on your ass, face, tits, legs, 6 packs. Good, now we can all sleep peacefully.

Pretty body and face without a beautiful heart are merely decoration.

What purpose do they serve?

Having a loving, gentle and kind heart, raw intelligence and a life of integrity. That's what beautiful means to me!

Other than that, what's the point? To be accepted by others? So they can be attracted to you? So they can like you? Is that what you want, to be liked because of your ass? Because of your physical appearance? Is that how you want to be valued? Wonderful, bravo!

126

"Do not compare your life to others!"

Do not compare yourself to others! You are unique and you have only one life.

Accept it the way it is, knowing that life is only as good as your mindset.

Maybe we can't choose our life situations, but we choose our mindset.

So, if someone says that you are taking the hard road, maybe they can't see that other option available was even harder!

Please don't take it personally, just keep walking... people don't know your reality or your life. They always assume things based on their perspective and based on image they have of you!

Your life, your choices, that's the only thing that matters!

127

"Sometimes you have to lose your mind to find your freedom!"

I wouldn't say that you have to lose your mind, but more to connect with yourself and follow your heart...

So, if you see that this is like losing your mind, then looooseee your mind freely, just find your freedom as well. Find your inner peace.

And freedom means being yourself.

And being yourself means speaking to yourself and finding your answer.

It's a process. change takes time.

128

"Maybe you're the girl that texts first who overanalyzes every message before sending wanting it to say exactly what's on her mind maybe you find yourself falling in love too easily or giving your heart away like it's a pin attached to your shoulder sleeve maybe you're the girl who has feelings for the boy who's unsure and you find yourself reading quote after quote about love wondering if you'll ever truly find it maybe you're the girl who has always cared too much putting everyone's else's heart before her own and maybe for once you need to stop apologizing for that"

Maybe.

If you are that woman/man (myself included), then listen, you beautiful soul:

Maybe you should start respecting the strength and the pure heart you have.

Maybe you should be focusing more on those who admire you for that.

Maybe you should be proud of yourself for having so much love to give.

Maybe you should realize that you are wonderful for putting your time and energy in picking your words so others could understand you.

And if they don't, never mind! You did your best, so you are not the one who is "losing" here.

Maybe you should start putting yourself before others, because maybe this time, you need it the most.

And please, stop apologizing for being real and start appreciating your values more!

The world needs more people like that.

129

"That was too close. I almost had to socialize."

I really love people, to meet some new great huuuumans, but I'm very picky about it.

I don't like to go out just because it's Saturday. I don't like to socialize just because 'everybody is going to be there'. I learnt to go with the flow and where I do feel good.

I like to spend time on my own, that's how I recharge, 'cause you know I need to be my best friend and all that socializing thing can be very exhausting.

130

"Be patient. Things will change for the better."

Patience, I guess, is one of those lessons that are most difficult to learn (at least for me).

It's important to learn, and so important NOT TO SAY to people who are experiencing some difficulties: be patient, things WILL change.

Instead just listen to them, try to understand and find the way to encourage and help them instead of giving them a formal reply! Sometimes even a hug helps.

Don't ask them how they are if you are not ready or open to listen to what they have to say.

It's as simple as that. Always think how would you feel in a situation like that. Even better, remember how you felt when you opened yourself to someone and you heard: *Smile, everything is going to be ok.* I'm sure we all have faced similar situations!

Instead, stay quiet or ask with the intention to truly listen and help.

This is essential for a good communication.

131

"Just be with me we'll figure out the details later."

This should be the right way of doing things. If you follow your heart.

People tend to overthink situations, possibilities, thinking only about what can go wrong. As a result, they often lose someone they really like. Fear is just a result of your own thoughts. Be aware of it.

And what if you just do that and go wherever your heart is? What if everything comes out just perfect? What if you risk all those things you are afraid of for love?

You see it's just a matter of perspective. Because you never know what will happen.

What matters is to be with that one you care about. What matters is that you follow your heart.

And all those things you fear of can be figured out.

So do risk... dare to risk.

In the name of love.

132

"When one door of happiness closes, another opens; but often we look so long at the closed door that we do not see the one which has been opened for us." – Helen Keller

Please think about this.

If one door closes, maybe it's because it is time for something better.

Maybe the door closes because there is no happiness behind them any longer.

And you do want that feeling of "happiness".

Therefore...

Maybe you should try paying attention to that another door that opens, maybe there is something waiting for you there. Step in, don't be afraid.

Usually, when we let go of something that was toxic for us, we create more space in our lives for something new and positive for us.

There's that.

133

"And in the middle of my chaos, there was you!" - Paullina Simons

Because sometimes, I believe that true love meets you in the middle of your mess, not your best. As the light at the end of the tunnel.

Keep your heart open, no matter what.

134

"Don't worry about what I'm doing. Worry about why you're worried about what I'm doing."

Why, ask yourself why? Your answer can really surprise you, but you have to be honest to yourself. (If you ever catch yourself worried about what someone else is doing, and it's not your loved one/s)

135

"When he wanted to take her picture, he didn't tell her to smile, but told her, "I love you" and her smile was more beautiful."

The real power and strength of a man is in the size of the smile of the woman he loves. Knowing how to treat and love her is the key. When a woman is loved by her man, it can't be hidden, she is more beautiful than ever and she can't give you anything but her best in return.

Just look into her eyes.

That's so rare to see nowadays.

136

"Don't let others project on you their fears, insecurities and prejudices."

Because it belongs to them!

Stop projecting your shit onto others!

Throughout my whole life, I was collecting other people's fears, doubts, without being aware of it. I was just wondering why are they telling me something, when I don't think that way?

For an instance, when I wanted to move to another country, the very moment I said that, I received tons of negative questions that made me regret I said it. Like: Why? What are you going to do there? Oh, you think that it's better there than here? And sooooooo on. But you got the point, right?

So even if I wanted to answer I wouldn't know what to say, since those were not actually real questions. Because I JUST WANT TO would be my answer.

You know, instead of being a philatelist I was a shitatelist. If you know what I mean...

Once I've learnt to recognise these things, I felt an enormous relief.

I've always wondered why people doubt you, why people discourage you, why people worry about you.

This last one worry about you is NOT THE SAME as caring about someone.

What I've learnt, this fucking speaks about them, not me! And quite often, they are not even aware of it. They just project their fears and insecurities on you. That's their way of being. It's their perspective, their limits, their beliefs, their education, their vision, their lives trying to project on you (with our without the intention to do so).

When that happens to me now... oh, boy...

137

"He calls me beautiful like it's my name."

This!

Anyone can call you beautiful, but what makes a huuuuuge

difference is WHO calls you beautiful and the meaning when they say that.

It's not about the word, but the tone, the intention, the way they look at you, the way they treat you! Beautiful is sooooo much more than a word.

138

"You should ask so you won't assume."

There is a great method called: asking.

I promise, it works.

Not just that it works, but it will save your time and energy, it will save you from overthinking, from creating possible and impossible scenarios, the list goes on... Especially in cases of you assuming something about someone.

God forbid that you speak to others about your assumptions about someone and you are wrong. That's gossip. And you even create a fake image of that person.

Do you see how wrong this can be?

Ask. Just ask. Save the planet and ask.

139

"You don't always need a plan bro'. Sometimes you just need balls."

Holy words...

Grow some balls bro' and dare to risk! No thinking, no planning, just do what your heart is telling you to do.

If you don't use your mind in the way it serves you, you will serve your mind. Overthinking, ruining possibilities with what ifs, maybes, with plan Bs, insecurities, fears, doubts, etc.

Please, do yourself a favour and read the second and third sentence again.

True love isn't found it's built.

140

"A woman doesn't just get up and leave you overnight. You've been fucking up for a while now bro'."

Nothing happens overnight bro'! But to make a decision to leave and actually leave can happen in just one second.

Instead of letting this happen, be sure that you nurture your relationship, of course, if you love your partner. Don't take them for granted, because one gets tired, you know?!

Where there is no love and one decides to leave because it's pointless to spend time in a relationship without love, respect and trust. This is the best-case scenario.

What usually happens is that partners cheat on each other instead of leaving each other. It is sooo easy, especially nowadays, where you are one click away from the virtual escape of your reality. With just one click you can ruin your life and the lives of others. Think before it's too late.

Thus, if you love your partner, nurture your relationship before it's too late. Don't let her/him go.

If you don't love each other anymore, be mature and responsible enough to sit down and talk in order to find a solution.

It won't be easy, of course, but that's the right thing to do.

141

"True love isn't found, it's built."

First and foremost, true love between the two is a must to have a healthy relationship.

You can't build anything if you don't (truly) love your partner.

Then you have to want to be there, things won't work by themselves unless you do.

The things you put in your relationship, they will grow.

Your energy, time, whether will you water it or not, because a relationship is like a flower.

You decide. Whether you will nurture it and build it or destroy it.

142

"It's all about finding calm in the chaos." - Donna Karan

It's all about this: mastering your thoughts and emotions.

Finding and keeping that inner peace no matter what. So, if you can't change your life situation, change the way you look at it, always reminding yourself that your inner peace is way more important than your current life situation.

To me, this was one of the most difficult things to learn... But as I said it before: practice, consistency, progression, not perfection.

143

"Fall in love with yourself first Then you can share that joy with someone else. Many of us are broken and looking for others to complete us or fill some void. No one can make you happy. That's an inside job." – Mark Sutton

I really try to pick the right words when I want to express myself and the word "broken" is not one of my preferences. What does it mean? We are all broken one way or another.

But you should definitely fall in love with yourself first. If you don't know how to love yourself, how can you expect from others to love you in the way you would like to be loved?

Then again, most of people look for others to complete them. Why? Again, you need the inner job instead. Learn to love yourself and you will see that you are already complete.

When you learn to love yourself:

Then you will be ready to have one happy & healthy relationship.

Then, you will be ready to share your love. And to receive it. In the right way.

Now go date yourself first and love yourself unconditionally.

144

"I had to forgive a person who wasn't even sorry – that's strength."

That's the real strength.

Forgiveness doesn't mean acceptance (approving) of other people's behaviour.

It means acceptance of the situation.

It means that we understand why they did something.

Forgiving others will give you peace.

Even if they don't feel sorry for what they've done.

145

"Some of the most generous people, have no money Some of the wisest people, have no education. Some of the kindest people were hurt the most." – Steve Wentworth

Because being generous has more to do with your time and

patience.

People very often think only about money as we live in a material world.

Being wise has absolutely nothing to do with education, but with life experiences.

People who were hurt the most know what kindness means when you need it the most.

Don't mix these things!

146

"I don't surround myself with people who are constantly positive, always smiling to mask the bullshit life they actually have. I prefer to surround myself with people who are real, honest & raw. If your day sucks, I want to hear about why it sucks so I can try my best to make it better. So if you're not really happy, don't fake a smile on my behalf. I'd rather you spill your guts with tears every day until your smile is real, because I don't care about the show the disguise, the political correctness. If you're in my life, I want you to be in your own skin."

I love real people! The same way I'm real.

I love people who dedicate their time for you, because they care for you.

I love people who genuinely and truly want to know how you feel, not those who ask you: how are you? so they can start a conversation, without really wanting to know how you are doing.

I love people who think before they use their words, who

impeccably use them so you can feel better or good about yourself. Those words that are dedicated just for you.

I love people who really try to understand what you have to say, not those who jump out to conclusions based on their own perspective.

I love people who are aligned with themselves so they talk what they think and do what they talk.

I love essentially genuine raw intelligent people who are not afraid of expressing themselves and how they feel.

Simply because I am a person who essentially cares about the essence, not the form.

147

"And if I could make you understand one truth, it would be this: someone who manipulates your feelings through guilt isn't loving you. that's an attempt to control you. And that has nothing to do with love."

If your partner doesn't want to break up with you, but you do for whatever reason, it can be very tricky to leave. Especially if they say that they love you, they can't live without you etc.

But, hey, first of all, you both deserve love.

If you are stuck in a toxic relationship, know that if your partner tries to manipulate you through feelings, emotions and tears... that's not love. That's manipulation. Selfishness.

If you stay in a toxic relationship because you think that you are doing a good deed, and if you think that staying loyal and committed to your toxic relationship is going to make you a good person. Think again. Neither of those two is true.You're mentally and physically exhausted, so you do what is easy. And you should be doing what is right.

You should stay loyal to yourself, not to the toxic environment and a manipulative person.

With this being said, you see that love doesn't exist there.

We all want love, right?

And if you are that one who tries to manipulate, I have one question for you: do you really want to be with someone who feels pity for you? You know, who looks at you like at a charity work?

148

"The most difficult thing we can learn is how to let go of our grudges for the poisonous people from the past. That's a great measure of courage."

And those are the most difficult lessons to apply! It takes true courage to do that. But don't forget that you do that for the better... better you, better life, better health. So... think again, is that really difficult? It's a beautiful thing to know that we are in charge, so take responsibility and take care of your life...

149

"Pain travels through family lines until someone is willing to heal it in themselves. By going through the agony of healing you no longer pass the poison chalice onto the generations that follow. It is incredibly important and sacred work."

Wow, when I saw this yesterday, I was blown away. Literally. Luckily, my mind still seems to work.

So, to all of you who feel and understand this quote...

I guess you will feel awake and isolated, like a black sheep of your family! You know, usually you are the one who recognises some pattern of behaviour that's not right.

I really encourage you to re-question all beliefs you have, which pass from generation to generation as a perfectly "normal" behaviour.

For instance, did you know that parents are quite ofthen the very first bullies to their kid?

What we accept as "normal" is sometimes not so normal. How will you recognize that? You will feel it.

As it's something I've been through and still "working" on that. Successfully, of course.

150

"I think it's very healthy to spend time alone. You need to know how to be alone and not be defined by another person." – Oscar Wilde

Oh, it is so important to spend some time alone!

For so many reasons.

You will learn so much about yourself.

How to love yourself, how to be your best friend, what you like and what you don't like. You'll learn how to listen to your heart and mind.

All those things are very important before we decide to be in a relationship.

People usually do the opposite. They look to others to complete them, to make them feel happy etc. And that's not how life works. No, no, no.

So... dig deep.

151

"Never forget who helped you out while everyone else was making excuses."

Never! But also don't forget those who are making fake excuses, knowing they could help, but not wanting to.

But, as usual – It goes the same vice vers. Do you catch yourself making excuses instead of helping?! Hmmm?

152

"The lamps are different, but the light is the same." – Rumi

We are all one, yet we are all different. We are simply unique, incomparable. You are you, I am I.

153

"Showing off is the fool's idea of glory." – Bruce Lee

Me, I'm very sensitive when I see things like that. Especially when they try to impress you with phones, cars... blah blah blah, and yet when they are empty inside. Or those who judge you based on the material things you possess.

'Some people are so poor, all they have is money.'

And the worst part is showing off. They are not aware of it. Because if they are...

154

"You can be a spiritual, empathetic, gentle, loving human being and still tell people to go fuck themselves when necessary." - Brooke Hampton

Holy fucking true. When necessary, simply because, sometimes that's the only way they can understand you.

Oh yes, pardon my French.

155

"The lesson is always love."

The answer is always LOVE.

156

We used to say: "Walls have ears". Now it's time to change the proverb to: "Ears have walls". - Paulo Coelho

I couldn't agree more!

Now walls don't need to have ears, because people share their privacy voluntarily through social media.

But ears do have walls. Paulo Coelho said it soooo well, so true!

Again, I love when people play with words for an effective result of simply to tell the obvious truth!

157

"The wound is the place where the Light enters you." — Rumi.

Kintsugi — When the Japanese mend broken objects, they aggrandize the damage by filling the cracks with gold. They believe that when something's suffered damage and has a history it becomes more beautiful.

Do not be ashamed of your wounds and scars. Heal them instead, that's what makes you who you are today. When you heal your wounds, you will shine even brighter than before.

158

"Someone once asked me how do you know if someone loves you and i told them it's in the way they look at you. A look that says they would hold back the ocean for you if they could." J. Iron Word

The way they look at you, the way they treat you, the way they make you feel... The one who loves you would never let you question all that!

159

"Why should a relationship mean settling down? Wait out for someone who won't let life escape you, who'll challenge you and drive you .... A relationship, with the right person, is a release not a restriction." - Beau Taplin

Who said that relationship means settling down? I mean, it doesn't matter who said it, what matters is: why did you ever accept that belief?

If settling down means: being with somebody who inspires you, who betters you, who makes you think, encourages you, who is there for you, who supports you and helps you in achieving your dreams and goals, who makes you feel good about yourself, who makes you smile and laugh... then ok, I'm fine with settling down.

And of course, as usual, act the same way. You deserve the love you give.

160

"Someone told me the other day that he felt bad for single people because they are lonely all the time. I told him that's not true I'm single and I don't feel lonely. I take myself out to eat, i buy myself clothes. i have great times by myself. once you know how to take care of yourself, company becomes an option and not a necessity." Keanu Reeves

Being lonely has nothing to do with being single. Or alone.

Way too many people who feel lonely are actually in relationships.

So, how's that?

Simply because in order to be in a relationship you have to learn to be happy alone. And people usually think that others will complete them, make them happy. So, when they don't receive what they want/need, they start feeling lonely.

As you can see, that's not how life works.

161

"Some talk to you in their free time, and some free their time to talk to you."

Never prioritize someone who treats you like an option!

And pay close attention...

Pay attention to the way people act when you're not doing well, pay attention to those who put their energy and time to contact you, who support you when you need it the most.

Pay attention to those who are loyal behind your back.

Pay attention to those who have constantly cared for you and your well-being, to those who genuinely want what's best for you.

Just pay close attention to those "small things" that make a huuuuge difference. Knowing the difference between people who deserve you and those who don't is everything.

162

"No matter how hard your life is, go to bed grateful you still have one."

Nothing is permanent. Life can be hard, but that's a part of the journey. Find things to be grateful for and try to shift your focus away from difficulties you're going through.

Try repeating this: my current situation is not my permanent situation. Or any other affirmative mantra that you find helpful.

163

"Place yourself where you can grow."

You are not a tree, so you CAN choose your environment!

In case that you can't change your current situation, people, try to focus on yourself and how to keep your inner peace, welcoming changes in the future.

164

"What would you do if you weren't afraid?"

Great question for a start of the day...

Know that fear is the product of your thoughts.

Also, know that there are 2 basic motivational "energies" that move you: love and fear.

Learn to understand which one drives you, because energy and what we believe in are so important when you do something.

If you believe that you will fail, most probably you will. Do it anyway. And learn something from that.

If you believe that you can do it, you would love to do it, but you are afraid, nervous etc. Do it. Just do it. Whether you fail or not, you will feel better afterwards. And you will learn something, definitely.

If you think about these two, you will notice the different energies. So why believing that you will fail?

165

"What will people say" This sentence has killed more dreams than anything else in the world.

Oh, yesss!

Living up to other people's expectations is not living your life, but allowing them to live your life.

Very often people are not aware of this. And they keep questioning even the smallest things.

For instance, quite often, people are afraid of going to the gym. Yet, very few ask themselves why, they rather block themselves with that fear. Because that's much easier.

And, their last escape is always: how will others look at them, what will they say.

And so on... women & make-up, beach body, putting on a bit of weight, etc. It's always that fear.

Got it?

166

"But sometimes you make a choice in that moment and you know in your heart it's going to change everything."

Every decision we make lead us to some change.

Decision we don't make is still a decision – that we don't want to decide.

Sometimes it takes true courage to take some risk, to decide and do something, because we are aware that nothing is going to be the same again. It feels scary, because we leave our comfort zone. Buuuuut if we are aligned with ourselves and we feel peace when we make that decision, no matter how scary it feels, that's the right thing to do... And SOOOOO worth it.

167

"Today I refuse to stress myself out about things I cannot control or change."

This should be everyday mantra. For everyone.

When you can't control what's happening, challenge yourself to control the way you react.

168

"Money doesn't make a man. Muscles don't make a man. Tattoos don't make a man. Character is what makes a man!" - Tony A. Gaskin Jr.

We live in the world of superficial values, where people value you based on what you have, or how you look, and not based on who you are.

But we all know that, right?

Hmm... that makes me think. I'm not sure whether we all know that you don't have to accept these values? I think that most of the people don't know that actually. You know, reality check.

So please, before you point your finger at others, make sure that you are not the same. It's time for some self-analysis.

169

"Anytime you have the urge to return to a harmful environment, keep in mind the damage it had on your sanity and the duration of time it took to regain your peace of mind." - Meggan Roxanne

Please keep this in mind!

And ask yourself why would you want something like that.

170

"The bible should be one sheet of paper, and on that paper, it should say: Try not to be a cunt, and if you do that every day, you'll be a good person." – Jim Jefferies

Okay, so let's continue this day with this beautiful inspirational quote.

And... Hey, don't be a dick!

It's that simple. Life is really simple.

Oh yeeeees, all you sensitive huuuuumans, please pardon my French.

171

"Protect your peace. Get rid of toxicity. Cleanse your space. Cultivate love."

Your body is your home. Your temple.

But don't wait for the spring to do some cleaning, to get rid of things you don't need. Do Feng Shui on daily basis.

Wipe all the dust from within, cleanse all toxicity you have accumulated and let yourself heal. Then seed some positive thoughts and let them grow.

Protect your inner peace and nurture your temple, always! Love yourself fiercely.

172

"If they abandon you when life gets hard, they never really loved you much at all."

The reason why and how they left you will tell you the truth. About them. About you.

You abandoned someone when life got hard? It's a sign of weakness.

And you, don't forget that it is always better to hear/see the truth than live a lie.

Know that they didn't love you the way you needed! The way you deserved! And the life won't be hard forever. Stay strong. For yourself. You need yourself.

173

"And then the day come when you met someone with a love so deep that the sun become the moon, and the moon become the sun, and you become yourself." - Simon B. Thomas

I wouldn't say that you become yourself, I would say that you finally feel peaceful because you will be accepted as you are and thus, you will be loved as you deserved.

So one day, you are going to meet someone for whom you will fall deeply in love.

174

"And then you came into my life…"

That one… Sometimes people come into our lives and you know right away they were just meant to be there.

Or you are that one who changes someone's life forever.

Hopefully for the better.

Isn't this beautiful?

175

"I used to think i was extremely introverted because I really liked being alone but it turns out I just like being at peace with myself and my surroundings & I am extremely extroverted when I'm around people who bring me comfort and happiness."

I didn't think I was an introvert even though I could relate to it. I love being alone and I enjoy 'me time'. But you know, I can relate to extrovert people too. I'm very open and communicative person.

So, what I wanted to say: I don't like labels! They really don't matter and can make a confusion. Rather listen to yourself and find what works for you. Find things you enjoy doing and do them often. Learn how to recharge your batteries, learn how to protect your energy, you know there are vampires out there. And not only because of and during Halloween.

176

"Those who died yesterday had plans for this morning. And those who died this morning had plans for tonight. Don't take life for granted. In the blink of an eye, everything can change. Forgive often and love with all your heart. You may never get to have that chance again."

Ufff...

You had a rough day? Well, maybe you should be grateful for being alive, healthy and for every breath you take... (every move you make...)

Do not take your life for granted. And do not take your life so seriously.

177

"Listen. I wish I could tell you it gets better. But, it doesn't get better. You get better." - Joan Rivers

Or bitter. You decide.

Life is full of ups and downs. Challenges and tranquillity. Love and loss.

It happens to all of us. That's life! Not good, not bad, but simply life.

And you, darling, you either get better or bitter.

178

"If your girlfriend/boyfriend isn't also your best friend, what's the point."

If you hide things from your partner, if you're looking for something on the side...

If you are not building and nurturing your relationship, if you don't trust your partner...

If you don't hang out with your partner, if you don't share your secrets...

If you don't speak about how you feel, if you don't go out on a date with your partner over and over again...

Then...

What's the point?

If your man/woman isn't your best friend... why are you together?

179

"For your mental and physical health if you can't improve your environment, you should leave it and save yourself." – S. McNutt

And again: Choose your peace over everything. You and your health should be your number one priority.

180

"Push yourself because no one else is going to do it for you."

When life hits you sooo fucking hard, remember this: It's not about who failed you down in your struggle, it is about who stayed by your side. It doesn't matter how many times you fall; what matters is how many times you stand up. It doesn't matter how hard life hits you, what matters is how much you can take and keep going forward. It's not about "friends" who left you during your difficult times, it is about beautiful people who helped you in your difficult times! Your focus determines your reality!

So when life hits you so fucking hard, your reaction will define you! You will either become a victim or stronger than ever before! It depends on you and you only. What you choose is what you become. So, who are you?!

I know who I am! Can you hear me screaming: THIS IS FUCKING SPARTAAAAAAAAA.

181

"The lesson: not everyone you love will stay. not everyone you trust will be loyal. Some people only exist as examples of what to avoid."

There are no coincidences in this life. People who cross our path are always there to teach us something. Lessons we have to learn.

You know like, when you meet someone and right away you know that you want to spend the rest of your life WITHOUT them? Yeah, exactly that.

182

"That first kiss."

I know that you are smiling while you're reading this, because you are thinking about someone and you know that there's nothing more magical than the first kiss with someone.

The best place in the world is inside a hug.

183

"Hiding your hurt only intensifies it. Problems grow in the dark and only become bigger and bigger. But when exposed to the light of truth, they shrink. You are only as sick as your secrets. So take off your mask. Stop pretending you're perfect. Walk into freedom." – Rick Warren

Think exactly like this.

When you struggle, and you're going through some tough period, but you're smiling, trying to hide it all, you will only feel worse, knowing that you're falling apart from within, but acting "happy" outside. Like that, you're simply not in alignment with yourself.

When you talk about how you feel with people who truly care for you, sometimes that's already enough to start feeling better. Sometimes you suddenly realise that you're overthinking, so speaking out your thoughts loudly, it can help you figure it out. Sometimes even a hug can help. Or a kind word. Or someone who will simply listen what you have to say.

Free yourself.

184

"A healer is someone who holds space for you while you awaken your inner healer so that you may heal yourself." – Maryam Hasnaa

Because no one can help you, unless you want to be helped. People motivate you, inspire you, but you are the one who needs to make decisions.

And you know, darling, sometimes you have to be your own hero!

185

"The problem with closed-minded people is their mouth is always open."

Do you ever wish you could just tell someone to "shut the fuck up"?

I do.

Sometimes or too often I get caught up in all kinds of situations. Let's just say I am surprised by the quantity of nonsense coming out from someone else's mouth. My facial expression speaks instead of me then. It makes me wonder why, oh why it is so difficult to make a connection between your brain and your mouth?

Yep...

The problem with the closed-minded people is that their mouth is always open.

Make sure your brain is connected to your mouth before you start talking.

186

"Birth --> In Between Stuff --> Death"

In between stuff – make sure you enjoy them. Your relationships, friendships, jobs, do not take your life too seriously.

I'm a very serious person who doesn't take life so seriously. (It's one of My quotes. Should I put my name under and make a photo as an evidence?)

187

"Our lives begin to end the day we become silent about things that matter." - Martin Luther King, Jr.

Silence usually means acceptance. Not approval.

One of the reasons why the world is a mess is not because of those who make rules, but because of those who accept them silently, even though they know deep inside they accept something that's not right.

By speaking up for yourself you also speak up for others. It's the same when you decide to stay silent.

Learn how to stand up for yourself. We need more of that.

188

"Everybody always asks if you have a career, if you're married, if you have children. Like if life was some kind of grocery list. No one ever asks us if we're happy." - Farrah Gray

The point of life is not about whether you have a great career, a university diploma, CEO in your job title, social status, kids or marriage.

The point is that you are fine even if you DON'T have anything from the list above.

The point is that you feel good from within.

So, create and check your list for living a happy and fulfilling life.

On the scale of 1 to 10 how good do you feel inside your skin?

May my every day be full of wisdom like today.

189

"If you're frustrated by something, is there a way to fix it?" - Richard Branson

Focusing on problem won't fix it, but it will cause frustration.

Rather look for the solution.

If you can't see the solution, don't get frustrated, it won't help!

Keep your inner peace and clear mind.

190

"Be with someone who makes adventures out of late-night trips to the grocery store be with someone who mindlessly reaches over for your hand while they drive be with someone who can't fall asleep without hearing your sleepy goodnight be with someone who brightens your monday and motivates you to do better be with someone who makes the stars seem to shine a little brighter."

You don't have to follow any of these if you don't feel like it, just be with someone who brings out the best in you!

Someone you feel comfortable with to share anything, your fears, dreams, thoughts. Someone who won't judge you or try to change you, but the one who will try to understand you and motivate your personal growth. Always for the better.

Someone with whom everything seems so easy: talking, spending time, you name it!

Someone from whom you will never feel the need to hide anything.

And vice versa! Because you two should be best friends.

191

"Things You Don't Need to Apologize for:

Loving someone. Saying "No". Following your dream. Taking "me" time. Your priorities. Ending a toxic relationship. Your imperfections. Telling the truth Standing your ground."

Please, don't ever apologize for being yourself!

BUT don't understand this literally, this doesn't mean you can be just anything.

For instance, if you do harm to others just because you THINK that you are being yourself.

No, honey, you are not being yourself, there are other various words to describe that kind of behaviour. Anyway, you should apologize and seek for the cause of your bad behaviour.

But never apologize for:

- Loving someone – never hide your emotions!

- Saying no – setting your limits is a part of self-care.

- Following your dreams – you should live up to your own expectations.

- Taking "me time" – as a part of the self-care routine.

- Your priorities – your life, your choices.

- Ending a toxic relationship – this is actually sooo beneficial for you and your health.

- Your imperfections – perfection doesn't exist. Try to be better, not perfect.

- Standing your ground – protect yourself and your dreams from anyone!

- Telling the truth – the truth above all. No matter how hard it is... just find the way to say it nicely.

Never apologize for any of these... Your life, your choices.

Do good to yourself and others but take no shit from anyone!

192

"Never trust your fears, they don't know your strength"
– Athena Singh

We go through our lives and make decisions based on the love or fear we feel. No matter how difficult it seems, don't let your fear guide you.

It's soooo important to learn the difference.

193

"Reflection cannot be seen in boiling water. Similarly, solution cannot be seen with a disturbed mind."

Great comparison!

Don't take permanent decisions based on your temporary mood. Whether you are angry, sad or upset, take your time & chill a bit before you decide what to do.

194

"Remember why you started."

When you face obstacles and before you decide to quit, just remember why you started in the first place!

For sure you will get tired, but that's not the reason to quit. Take a break, learn how to rest, not to quit.

If you feel like you want to quit, it should be when you are on top, not when you feel tired.

So, wait for that good day and ask yourself the same question. Then you will be able to see the difference between being tired and wanting to quit.

Also, remember those who believed in you! Who were there. Support. If there was any. If there was not any, remember that you must believe in yourself. Always.

195

Mac MacGuff: "Look, in my opinion, the best thing you can do is find a person who loves you for exactly what you are. Good mood, bad mood, ugly, pretty, handsome, what have you, the right person is still going to think the sun shines out your ass. That's the kind of person that's worth sticking with." – Juno (2007)

This.

Just the way you are. The same way you should accept and love someone just the way they are.

Because love is not when you love just parts of someone. That usually means that you love that parts for how they make YOU feel. Not for who they are.

196

"Everyone thinks of changing the world, but no one thinks of changing himself." - Leo Tolstoy

The golden rule: When you start pointing fingers, point them at yourself first.

Change always starts with you. Whether we talk about yourself or about the world. Be that change you wish to see in others.

197

"I respect those that tell me the truth, no matter how hard it is."

Can someone remind me please: What's the point of believing in lies? What's the point of lying? What's the point of living in a lie?

Yes, some truths are difficult to say, to speak about, to live. But will telling the lie make them better, easier? No.

People very often hide behind excuses like: Oh, he or she will get angry or upset. And that's why they tell lies. This is selfish and not right. You should do what is right, and let other person process things in their own way. Your job is to tell the truth.

The truth above all.

198

"A relationship isn't always 50/50 Some days, they will struggle. You suck it up and pick up that 80/20 because they need you. That's love."

And some days you will struggle too. And you will be able to give only 20%, so you will need those 80%.

Because that's what love is.

Because 1+1=1

199

"He who does not understand your silence will probably not understand your words." - Elbert Hubbard

There are some people who could hear you speak a thousand words and still not understand you. And you will repeat the same words trying to explain yourself, over and over again. But they still won't understand you. Even though you explained yourself perfectly.

The same way they won't understand your silence.

Simply because we all hear and understand each other through the filters of our own perspective. Our own depth. Our own consciousness and so many other things that include: beliefs, education, experiences...

And then, there are some people who will understand you, your silence, your everything.

Because they know how to "read" you, your energy and everything about you.

This is extremely rare. Keepers.

200

"Pain and adversity are powerful vehicles to promote personal growth. Nothing helps you learn, grow, and evolve more quickly. Nothing offers you as big an opportunity to reclaim more of your authentic power as a person." - Richard Bach

Rumi's quote: the cure for pain is in the pain.

So many wise people out there... I love it!

Yet, we live in a very superficial world, but it's up to you, you choose your focus. My choice is to learn, to grow, to serve/ help and share my knowledge. I live in the world of mediocrity and superficial values, yet there's nothing superficial about me.

How is this possible? Simply, I refuse to accept (as a part of my life) anything that doesn't resonate with me.

As I said... you create your life by making right decisions.

201

"You can eat Kale, drink alkaline water, take vitamins and do yoga... but if you don't deal with the shit going on in your heart and head... you're still unhealthy"

Being healthy is so much more than going to the gym and eating healthy whole foods.

If you don't deal with shitty situations in your life, you nurture negative emotions within yourself and that reflects on your health!

It's like planting a seed of negativity, so don't expect to grow something positive out of it.

Suppressing how you feel is extremely self-destructive.

202

"I think every week should have one day in it when BOYS give presents to GIRLS." - Lucy van Pelt (Peanuts)

I couldn't agree more! At least once per week...

C'mon boy(s), show love to your girl and just how much you care. Not just on special occasions/dates. It's all about giving. Surprise her. And she will give you back 10x more.

It all starts with boys. It is simple as that. That's how life works. Biology as well, and I don't mess with biology.

203

"You know we're not put on this earth to live perfect lives."

... but rather to live our lives, which is perfect enough.

There's no such thing as perfect people, perfect life, perfect looks, perfect relationships.

We will get hurt, we will hurt, we will be loved, we will love. That is all life.

But... There is a life, people, etc. that is/are perfect FOR YOU. Which depends on you, thus define what is perfect life FOR YOU.

But before you do that, make sure that: You come as you are. Real. Perfectly imperfect. And don't compare yourself or your life to others. Then you will be able to find your perfect.

204

"People will quit on you. You gotta get up every day and make sure you never quit on yourself."

They will!

But who cares! You? People who quit on you shouldn't be a reason of your sadness. Ask yourself why would you put the key of your happiness in their hands? Why would you depend on others?

Accept that people come and go. The same way you appear and disappear from someone's life. Yes, it can hurt, yes it can be difficult.

But...

Don't quit on yourself, no matter how hard it is. Never! You should be your best friend, and best friends don't quit!

205

"Interesting how love finds you when you stop trying to find it."

Simply because you let go of "needing someone".

You realise that you WANT that one, but you DON'T NEED them.

When you feel comfortable in your solitude, when you learn how to love and respect yourself, your time, you will be able to let go of that feeling that you need someone.

And when you least expect it, love will come.

206

"He said "You are beautiful". I told him "beautiful is a lazy and lousy way to describe me"" - Ijeoma Umebinyuo

Someone's effort reflects their interest in you!

How someone treats me is what matters to me. That genuine words and pure intentions. So, if you are going to treat me like an ordinary person, like every other person you speak to... naaah... it's not a good start, as I am everything, but ordinary.

Not modest, but self-aware. We should be all thinking this way, as we are all unique, so why generalize?

207

"Mindfulness is simply being aware of what is happening right now without wishing it were different; enjoying the pleasant without holding on when it changes (which it will); being with the unpleasant without fearing it will always be this way (which it won't)." - James Baraz

Let's silent our chattering thoughts and simply be aware of this moment. Whatever you do, wherever you are, try to be present. Now. Without thinking about yesterday or tomorrow, or anything that you are going through.

Fill your mind with kindness to yourself and to your body. Know that nothing is permanent, and that every problem has a solution.

208

"Being a human was the hardest thing I've ever had to do."

We are all humans. Yeah, pfffff, mind-blowing, I know...

Yet it is so rare to spot humanity among humans.

We have a common sense for reason, yet it's so rare to see human beings using it.

In the right way, for the right purposes.

No wonder that it is difficult to be a human.

So, you dear huuuuuman, are you really human?

209

"Would you like you, if you met you?"

A question of the day.

Something to think about, because it is a great question for self-analysis.

The benefits of self-questioning:

- It's great for self-reflection

- It helps you progress

- It helps you grow

- It helps you find a solution

- You can learn so much about yourself

And so on...

Asking yourself the right question is very important.

210

"You aren't what's happened to you, you are how you've overcome it." - Beau Taplin

You know, life can really surprise you with both good and less good things. Usually, it's not up to you. I can tell you that.

But how you react when something happens, yes that IS up to you.

Your attitude and your decisions will shape you, just as your personality and your mindset, and they will definitely craft your life. Your future.

So, learn how to rule and control your mind. Your mind is a very powerful tool.

211

"The things you hide in your heart.... eat you alive."

Literally.

Just talk about how you feel. No matter how difficult or stupid it may sound, find a way to express yourself, always!

No ifs, no buts, no maybes, just do it.

By leaving feelings and thoughts unspoken, you will just accumulate everything and after a a while, it's going to feel like a burden, which you will drag around on your back. In this way, you're also creating a bad habit so you will start behaving the same way in various different situations.

Do I even need to mention that it can reflect on your health and your well-being?

You like someone? Tell them.

Somebody makes you feel uncomfortable? Tell them.

You feel unhappy? Speak about that with people who care.

You need to take a break? Express that.

And so on, it applies to whatever you are going through.

212

"Big brave heart it is okay to feel scared too." Leah Stone

Because the absence of fear is not a sign of courage. Courage is the ability to keep going in spite of fear.

You can be strong and afraid in the same time.

You can be independent and still need support.

You can be a leader but still need some guidance.

You can be direct and straightforward but also kind at the same time.

You can be the one who understands others but still set clear boundaries.

So those who say: I'm not afraid of anything...

Let me tell you something: there's no such thing.

213

"We get so worried about being pretty. Let's be pretty kind. Pretty funny. Pretty smart. Pretty strong." - Britt Nicole

First and foremost, worrying doesn't take away any problem.

But if you do worry anyway...

How about this: instead of being so worried about superficial and material things...

Try worrying about whether you've been kind enough? To yourself and to others.

You should be kind. Pretty much kind.

Have you done something good today? For yourself and for the others?

This world would be so much better if we would stop worrying about being pretty and worry more about being valuable for what we are beyond our physical body.

Hmmm?

214

"I reward love with loyalty & doubt with distance. It's never complicated."

It is as simple as that!

I'm pretty much transparent and I usually speak out whatever I think. You know, this blonde head needs to be in alignment with herself.

Things in life are pretty simple. Life is pretty simple.

People complicate everything.

215

"Stop making stupid people famous."

Please!

Though, maybe calling someone "stupid" is not what I would say.

I would say stop making people with no true values famous.

Whether you talk about them in a negative or a positive context, all the same.

Either way, you give them publicity. And as you might know, any marketing is a good marketing.

Moreover, if you post something calling someone "stupid", what does that say about you? That you are 'being smart' by posting things with no value and by calling someone stupid?

I'm always keen on pointing things out, but only IN THE RIGHT WAY.

Focus on those with true values and promote them. Use social media to impact people positively.

Stop promoting people with no values. Please!

216

"Go for someone who is not only proud to have you, but will also take every risk just to be with you."

This. Risk everything for love and don't accept anything less than you deserve.

Actually, let me put it this way... you deserve the love you give.

The same amount you give, the same effort. So, you know the answer...

217

"Train your mind to be calm in every situation."

The hardest lesson to learn! But immensely important for good health and overall wellbeing.

Try to add some new habits and maybe some of these can help:

− make a step-by-step plan to reach your goal,

− try to be grateful for what you have,

− make jokes about life and situations in general,

− try to disconnect and step back so you could decompress and refocus your thoughts,

− try to have a good night sleep because that's how your brain literally recharges.

And if the real cause of stress in your life are people, try to understand why. By asking yourself the right questions, you will find the answer. If you have doubts about what kind of questions you need to ask yourself, ask for a professional help. There is nothing wrong with that. Usually, people are like our mirrors, so it is very important to know why some people are causing us stress.

And: practice, practice...

218

"Help people even when you know they can't help you back."

You know, I am a kind of person who likes to pick the right words to describe or define something. So, when I see some quote or definition or description which makes the wrong point, well let's just say that I need to point it out.

This is one such example.

You might not see anything wrong with the statement above. But read my opinion first.

Help people EVEN when you know...

EVEN? I mean, seriously?

First of all, any kind of help should always be without any calculations. We should all help each other. At least, when we are in a position to help. Help doesn't require helping back. It should simply be a voluntary action, knowing that we could make a difference in someone's life.

Sometimes, we will also need help.

Helping while expecting something in return is not help, but business.

Isn't it hard enough to feel that you need some help? When you need to ask for help?

So why putting more misery onto that? Think about this, please.

Let's make each other's lives easier.

This quote should have only two words: Help people.

Namaste.

219

"And you, you scare people because you are whole all by yourself." - Lauren Alex Hooper

Yeah, yeah, I know, but that's none of my business.

Remember this: if people are intimidated by your strength, that's just a reflection of their weakness. So, they will try to drag you down, to break your spirit. That is still their weakness, learn to recognize this. Don't let that affect you.

Be kind (to yourself) and step away. Let them fight their own battles.

220

"How to say fuck you in a nice way?"

I'm giving a shout-out to all the people who (are trying to) use words impeccably. Who pick their words carefully when they want to say something.

Who think before they speak, but who also use the F word (me included) without causing harm to others.

The F word is quite a magical and powerful tool to release stress.

221

"The problem is people are being hated when they are real and are being loved when they are fake." - Bob Marley

But don't take their hate personally, people will hate you for being real just because you are all they want to be, but they are not. You are like a mirror to them. You remind them of what they are not. And behind that hate is actually a huge admiration.

The same people will admire and love those "fake ones". Again, they are like a mirror to them.

Be real. Stay real. Always.

Always remember someone's effort is a reflection of their interest in you. how they treat you is how they feel about you.

222

"When you realize it's not personal, there is no longer a compulsion to react as if it were." – Eckhart Tolle

It took some time for me to understand this in the right way. A blonde thing, I guess.

I'm still trying to apply it. Some days I fail, some days I don't.

What people see in you is reflection of themselves, also what you see in others is reflection of yourself. As we are looking in the mirror. How we see others speaks about us.

Don't get drained.

Always think about your inner peace and how to keep it. Understanding and accepting things, people as they are.

When I struggle to "understand" them, I try to remember and repeat this: This is not my circus, these are not my monkeys.

223

"When someone walks away from you, it's not the end of your story. It's the end of their character's role in your story."

People come and go. Life continues with or without them. They come for a reason the same way they walk away for a reason. The same way you have walked away from someone's life. Hmm, you did, as we all did, and we all know our reasons.

So, think about this, it can be very helpful.

It can be difficult and it will be difficult but close the chapter anyway, knowing that in every end, there is also a new beginning.

224

"Ladies, a man that is truly interested in you will never leave you guessing about the role he intends to play in your life. Good men pursue the women that they WANT WITH UPFRONT COMMUNICATION GENUINE INTENTIONS AND CONSISTENT EFFORT."

When a man is truly interested in you, there will be no need for you to do the pursuing. He won't make excuses, he will be determinate in his intention of having you in his life. Men are born to pursue and conquer women. Not vice versa. It is in our DNA, and I don't mess with biology.

And to both: Ladies & Gentlemen (no difference here, the same goes for both women and men), games are for immature people who lack self-confidence & self-esteem. Playing with other people's emotions is an act of selfishness & cowardness.

225

"Life is not a competition. Life is about helping and inspiring others so we can reach our potential."

The only person you should compete with is you and who you were yesterday, because...

We are here to help each other to get through this life. Life can be unpredictable, but your help shouldn't be.

We are here to be kind to each other. We can disagree over the same thing, but kindness, kindness should be always present. If you think that grass is greener on the other side, maybe it's because you were focusing on their grass, instead of focusing and nurturing your own.

Or maybe their grass is fake. Who knows. But this shouldn't

bother your head at all. Look at your grass and nurture it. That's where your focus should be.

And if you need some help, ask your neighbour for some advice, maybe it will be helpful.

226

"If it cost you your peace it's too expensive. This includes people, places and things." Manuela Escobar Leguízamo

1. Health

.

.

.

2. Health

.

.

3. No money in the world can buy your health

4. No money in the world can restore your inner peace

5. Let go of anything that steals your dreams

6. Toxic people need to get out of your life

7. Your health is priceless and should be your number 1 priority

8. Self-love. Self-talk.

227

"Real love doesn't meet you at your best. It meets you in your mess." - J.S. Park.

Very true...

Not when everything goes smoothly. No, no, no.

The one who stays by your side when you are a mess. The one you feel comfortable with, with whom you can open yourself when you are most vulnerable. To feel "naked".

The one who supports you to get back on track.

The one who will motivate you and prioritise you simply because you need it.

The one who won't judge but try to understand your situation so he/she could help.

The one who will pick up your pieces back together.

The one who will see your true self.

The one whose hugs feel like a home.

That's how you will know that he/she is there for you.

Hopefully all these "the one" won't be different ones, but only one! The only one.

228

"I built me."

And... no one can take that away from me.

Working on yourself is the best investment and the best thing you can do for yourself in your life.

You can build a house, you can have a perfect job, you can invest in material things, and you can lose it all in just one second. I know that. I've been there.

Life is our only teacher. We are all students.

You can't avoid or ignore life. But yes, you can choose to ignore your personal growth.

Learning, pushing yourself and your limits, confronting your fears, stepping out of your comfort zone, everything leads you to: Your personal growth. Fulfillness. Things become so much clearer. Simple, as they should be. You become a wiser, better person, to yourself and to others. Sharing what you have learnt so others can learn too.

It's up to you. You can build yourself or you can destroy yourself. You can reach higher levels of consciousness or you can stay on the same level where you were 10 years ago.

Forever and always – you decide.

And I, I built ME. By myself. And no one can take that away from me. Ever.

229

"It's a miracle we ever met."

Have you ever thought about how and why you met persons who were (are) important to you?

Have you ever met someone you immediately felt a strong connection to?

Isn't it wonderful?

Or when you meet someone and you feel that you want to spend the rest of your life without them?

In my humble opinion: Coincidences don't exist!

I think that we all "recognise" each other by our energies. The same way we attract each other. Your energy never lies, it introduces you before you say a word.

We meet people for a reason.

Life works in mysterious ways, but it's only up to us to discover the reason why.

230

"You will suddenly meet the right person. Suddenly your health will improve. Closed doors will open, new relationships will blossom, goals will be reached, and prayers will be answered."

The same way suddenly everything hits you.

You end your relationship, quit your job or get fired, you lose someone, you let go of friends and so on. You know, one day you have it all and the next day you have nothing.

But that's all life. Ups and downs.

No matter where you are at this point, remember that everything is temporary.

All we can do is go with the flow, accept and adapt. Learn and grow.

Believe. In yourself.

Life is full of waves and we need to learn how to surf. Practice patience...

231

"Don't let your mind play tricks on you. Overthinking and worrying is the cause of unnecessary pain."

Your mind is a very powerful tool!

Be aware and watch over your thoughts.

Pick your thoughts wisely. Those that serve you.

Let go & focus on what you can change.

Rule your mind or let your mind rule you.

232

"Don't move the way fear makes you move. Move the way love makes you move. Move the way joy makes you move." – Osho

We move through life based on how we feel and usually there are two basic feelings: love or fear.

When fear moves you, you can't progress, but pull back from life.

When your decision is based on love, you are open to new beautiful things. And you will keep progressing.

But first and foremost, you (should) learn what love is. How to love yourself, and when you learn that, you will be able to love others.

233

"Because in the end, you won't remember the time you spent working in the office or mowing your lawn. Climb that goddamn mountain." – Jack Kerouac

To travel is to live.

Travel is something that makes you richer. In so many ways.

One of my goals is to travel as much as I can. As long as I can.

As far as I can.

To collect memories, not things, to meet new people, cultures. To enrich my soul and open new horizons.

234

"It's the maybes and what-ifs that will kill you."

Being indecisive is something that can create your anxiety. So easily. Overthinking, overanalysing about pros and cons.

The most important thing is to listen to your guts when you need to decide about something. Guts know what is good for you, it's your true self.

Then decide. And stick to your decision without thinking about other options you had.

No maybe, no what if... No, no, no.

Ask yourself the right questions and listen to what your heart is telling you. There lies the answer.

And if you still have doubts about two choices, try this, it always works.

Visualise each side of the coin for one of your two choices. Then flip the coin. You will know the answer already while the coin is in the air. If not, then cover it with your hand without looking at it and think about which result you hoped for.

Decide. AND DO IT. No matter how difficult it feels. And seems. Do it.

Your heart never lies, unlike your mind.

235

"Start by doing 1 push up Start by drinking a cup of water Start by paying toward 1 debt Start by reading 1 page Start by making 1 sale Start by deleting 1 old contact Start by walking 1 lap Start by attending 1 event Start by writing 1 paragraph Start today Repeat tomorrow We all start somewhere!"

Before you start, set those "goals" – what would you love to do but you think you have no time.

It could be anything.

Then decide when you will start.

Write it down and put it in a visible place, like a reminder.

You should commit to yourself.

And start.

Then repeat it until it becomes a habit.

236

"When you realize you only feel powerless because you keep giving your power away to people who don't deserve any of your precious fucks."

First and foremost, you have to acknowledge this.

I know...

It's really frustrating when you realise this, but hey, it's always better late than never.

Why? Because no matter how frustrating it can be, you are in charge and you can change it.

So save yourself from more frustrations.

You don't need any more shit.

Know that it's up to you where you let your energy flow, pay attention to where your attention goes. The same direction your energy will follow. These things will grow.

Be mindful about this.

237

"Whatever just wash your hands."

Is it really that difficult?

Please. Wash. Your. Hands.

Inform yourself about diseases and possible consequences coming from not washing hands.

Maybe this is needless to say to some of you, to lots of you, I hope. If you are one of them, congratulations. You are doing well for yourself and for others.

Maybe to some of you this sounds, funny, and obsolete, but I'm amazed with how often people forget this. That's some lack of basic education/manners.

Please wash your hands.

238

"I do not crave anyone who will fix me. Just someone who will hold my hand while I fix myself."

I think that we all crave and need this.

That's how it should be.

The one who will be there, understanding and supporting you. And holding your hand while you go through some shitty situations, letting you heal.

The same way we will hold someone's hand.

And "fix" is not the word I would use, rather heal and improve.

239

"You can't skip chapters, that's not how life works. You have to read every line, meet every character. You won't enjoy all of it. Hell, some chapters will make you cry for weeks. You will read things you don't want to read, you will have moments when you don't want the pages to end. But you have to keep going. Stories keep the world revolving. Live yours, don't miss out."

You simply can't avoid life and escape things that hurt.

I mean, of course you can, most people actually do that. They don't go through their shit by dealing with it, they escape from it by looking for some temporary remedies. Drinking, smoking, drugging, cheating, and so on.

There is nothing wrong with having a drink every now and then, but only if you do it to enjoy yourself.

First and foremost, if you don't face your problems, you will continue carrying them to your present, future and you will share it with other people who don't deserve your shit. You know what I mean, right?

That's why this world is full of people walking around miserable and passing their frustrations to others. Nice gifts.

And you wonder why this happens? Why someone is throwing their frustrations at you? Well, you will find the answer above.

So...

Go through it. Give yourself time. Cry. Allow yourself to feel everything. Connect and talk to yourself in order to find a solution. Talk to others if you have some issues. Just sit down and say, "Let's fix this".

Keep this in mind: not all positive changes feel positive and easy at the beginning.

They laugh at me because I'm different, I laugh at them because they are all the same. your uniqueness is your gift.

240

"Your diet is not only what you eat. It is what you watch, what you listen to, what you read, the people you hang around. Be mindful of the things you put into your body emotionally, spiritually and physically."

Literally. You can eat avocados and kale, drink smoothie, but if you surround yourself with toxic people, if you feed your mind with toxic thoughts, if you nurture your soul with toxic partner, then all avocados of this world will not help you stay healthy.

Be mindful about this.

241

"The sad truth is many people are in love and not together and so many people are together but not in love."

Why, oh, why?! Are you one of those people who use excuses to stay in a relationship with no love, just because you are afraid of...?

- what others will say?

- a new start?

- being alone?

- taking a risk?

Do you use your children as an excuse?

Again, why, oh, why?

What is more important than your own happiness (and your partner's happiness)? If you are not happy, what kind of example do you give to your kids? What other people will say? WHO CARES! You believe change won't be easy?

What makes you think that living without love is easier?

Isn't it already painful?

242

"Not everyone will like you, and that's completely okay."

Life lessons. I've always said this: If everybody likes you, you are doing it wrong.

Firstly, I don't need to be liked or loved. Respect is a must. Secondly, "no one is more hated than the one who speaks the truth". Thus, I love to speak the truth no matter what...

Thirdly, what matters to me is quality, not quantity. My focus is on those people who accept me for who I am and on those I can help. I am not here to please everybody and live by their expectations, but to live MY life doing the things that make me feel HAPPY. Therefore, not everyone likes me, but not everyone matters.

Not everyone will like you, and you don't have to give a shit.

243

"Create a life that feels good on the inside, not one that just looks good on the outside."

Way too many people strive to have good cars, good clothes, material things in general, thinking that these things will bring them happiness. Yet, they remain so unhappy.

Let me help. What we are looking for is that feeling when we buy something we like, not the shoes we buy. That excitement. That's why so many people equalize buying with happiness.

Don't get me wrong, I like nice stuff, we all do. But it has nothing to do with happiness. Happiness is an inside job. Way too many people who are posting photos of "good life" are trying to impress others with how well they live, yet they forget to impress themselves with things that nurture their souls.

They just don't know how to be happy. Superficial world we live in is to be blamed and things that our society is teaching us.

That's a sad reality, but also a wakeup call. All this can change, if we are willing to change.

244

"Don't admire people too much. They might disappoint you."

OMG, just one of so many things that you can find on internet, and hopefully, you won't believe it.

This is so NOT true!

Why?

It is not people who disappoint us, but the expectations we create!

The thing is that we have certain type of expectations from people – how we would like them to behave, instead of seeing and accepting them for who they are. We all have some kind of expectations.

And booom! Once they fail your expectations, you will say oh, they disappointed me. Well, noooo, you're wrong.

They can "disappoint" you in case they don't keep their word, or do something knowing it will hurt your feelings. Even then, that shouldn't stop you from admiring others.

I will always admire people who inspire and motivate me! Never stop admiring people with true values! Expect nothing, but respect...

245

"If your friend owns a business, support them by buying their product.... not asking for something for free all of the time."

You know, any kind of support they need.

Depending on their business. Encourage them! Be a friend. Support is not just money. But if they sell something, why don't you buy their product like a Christmas or a birthday gift for someone? If they are good in something, and promote real values, sharing their work or spreading a word is also a support.

I had to learn that the hard way. I guess like any other thing in my life. Because of my expectations that every single person will behave like I would! I thought they were my friends, so that it should be a normal thing to support me. Like I (did) support them. But that's not how life works.

You'll know who your real friend is when you need that support. I definitely do know... now.

246

"Distance doesn't separate people... Silence does." – Jeff Hood

Good and healthy communication is essential for any kind of relationship. Among other things, good communication is feeling comfortable to say whatever is on your mind in a respectful way, of course.

Then distance can't separate two hearts. Distance can't stop love. Distance serves like an excuse for breaking up, and usually behind those excuses is fear of commitment, maybe even the lack of love, etc.

Lack of communication in a relationship can lead to separation whether your partner is miles away or by your side. The greatest distance between two people is misunderstanding. Sometimes, the biggest distance is when you feel distant from your partner under the same roof. You probably know that silence full of unspoken questions, a heavy silence. Feeling apart while living together can be destructive, while effective communication can overcome any challenge, even a long distance.

As you can see, it is not about distance but about what creates a distance.

But it takes two for tango. 1+1=1

247

"No one is too old for fairy tales."

You know, you live what you believe in. Or you will end up believing what you live. It is all about believing, defining and creating.

I believe that life is supposed to be like a fairy tale. You should live your own fairy tale, depending on what fairy tale means to you. If you believe in fairy tales. Maybe you believe in something else. Or maybe you will name your life differently. The name doesn't matter, but believing does.

Me, I believe in magic, miracles, unicorns, eternal pure love, so yes, that's my own little world, my fairy tale. My Narnia.

248

"The truth is that airports have seen more sincere kisses than the wedding halls, and the walls of hospitals have heard more prayers than the walls of a church."

... and dead people are getting more respect than those alive.

Very true! What does this say? We live in a world full of hypocrisy? No common sense out there.

Will going to the church make you a better person?

Does staying (getting) married to someone you don't love make you a sincere person?

I always love to say, it's not about the form but about the essence.

What is essential is what really matters. Essence doesn't change.

It's love.

When you believe.

Form? Forms come in different "shapes" and usually represent some rules that someone invented merely to simplify life (I hope so) and they are usually blindly accepted by society.

Following forms without essence won't make you a good person, but just one of millions who follow some rules blindly, without questioning, without using any common sense.

So if you want to follow some type of form, make sure that you are doing it for the right (essential) reasons.

And make sure that you bring some value to the world...

249

"There is a voice inside of you that whispers all day long, 'I feel that this is right for me, I know that this is wrong.' No teacher, preacher, parent, friend or wise man can decide what's right for you - just listen to the voice that speaks inside." - Shel Silverstein

Listen to that voice that comes from within, that's your true self. Shutter your mind and listen to your heart, it knows the way.

Life is our teacher and we are all just students, learning from situations that life gives us.

Listen to your gut feeling, it never lies.

And if your gut tells you that something smells fishy, then it probably does stink.

Likewise, if something makes your heart jump in joy, or you feel butterflies in your stomach, your body speaks for a reason, follow that feeling...

Trust your guts!

250

"There are things in life that will threaten to dim your light. Use them as a fuel to shine brighter! - Princess Sassy Pants

There are those kinds of people who will try to convince you that you are not happy, even though, you tell them you are doing just fine.

Or those who tell you that you are doing something wrong. Or those who don't understand how you can say that you are fine if you are going through some difficult times?

Well, yes, it is possible. And they don't understand it.

Or those who will panic for you when something stressful happens. And who will try to pass that panic to you by asing additional questions like: *But how can you stay calm?* or *don't you worry about that?*

No, dear, I'm only worried that I will slap you in the face for not leaving me alone.

Or those who will tell you that you can't do something just because they think they can't.

You know them? Yeah, me too. Please, stay away from them. Your peace is more important than anything in the world.

251

"The more you learn the more you see."

Learn new things every day!

Invest in your knowledge!

We live in the world of modern technology and thanks to internet you can learn new things FOR FREE.

Only if you want to... you are just one click away from different kind of tutorials, lessons... just pick whatever you are interested in.

What I listen soooo often is that internet is something bad and people who blame internet for divorces, cheating etc.

And I'm like, shocked. People are not aware of what they are talking about. They are not awake.

Well let me tell you, it is not about internet but you and your choices.

I'm so grateful for having that possibility to connect with likeminded people from all over the world. To learn things interesting to me or things I need. And for so many other things that internet has brought us!

As you can see, internet is an escape for someone and a veeery useful tool for someone else.

Think before you speak, be mindful before you click and OPEN YOUR MIND, that's how it works!

252

"When the roots are deep, there is no reason to fear the wind." - African Proverb

Knowing that we all live based on our beliefs, make sure that your beliefs serve you. Always try to find the things that ground you, simply because when you know who you are, when you have your values, when you have integrity, nothing can really break you.

The wind will come, that's just a part of the life. One breeze or typhoon here and there can bend you just for a second or a minute, but after that, you will come back to stand up tall once again and you will firm your roots even better, even deeper...

Be brave, you have the power.

253

"It's hard to be a woman. You must think like a man, act like a lady, look like a young girl, and work like a horse."

This made me smile, but also also made me think.

Yeah, I know, we live in men's world, but I know women who think like men and have the strength of men (in business and life)

and men who act like women. I like to say, if there is anything worse than a hysterical woman, it would have to be a hysterical man. And, trust me, I know them.

I don't think that it is hard to be a woman. But, oh boy, living in this world, yes, it can be hard.

I don't want to think like a man, I think as a human being, as Irina.

I don't need TO ACT like a lady, 'cause I AM one.

I don't want to look like a young girl. I am a woman. And again, it is the pressure that woman feels that she needs to look like a 20-year-old girl.

Working like a horse? I'm not a horse. I'm very feminine.

I am a woman who likes to feel like a woman in a man's company. To be treated like a woman. But living in a men's world, yes, a woman has to work twice as much so she can "earn" respect.

As you can see, it is not difficult to be a woman, but the world we live in gives us some hard times. Do we live in a world of feminized men and women who are competing and comparing to those men? Yes! But I don't accept it. I don't mess with biology and DNA... no, no, no.

254

"Energy cleansing is not a glamorous process.

It is not about good vibes, yoga and buddha bowls.

It's heavy, deep and can feel very ugly.

Most people like to pretend healing is just about magic and positive vibes.

Healing is accepting + integrating painful experiences from the past.

Honesty and transparency are important.

Allow yourself to feel whatever you feel, and don't hide it.

Don't be ashamed of it ever."

The same way you clean your home (I hope you do), you should be cleaning your body from all the negativity.

And I don't mean detox juices and stuff, but digging deep within you. Self-talk, self-analysis to find an answer why something bothers you or gives you anxiety, frustration, stress, sadness.

Not an easy process, but so important for your health.

And to all you who read this nodding or rolling your eyes, great, I hope you are fulfilled and satisfied with your life.

255

"First it hurts then it changes you."

Pain changes us.

Pain is an opportunity for personal growth. And it changes our perspective.

Pain can either make you stronger or make you weaker. It only depends on you.

There are two types of pain.

The first one is inevitable, what life brings you. Pain that hurts. This type of pain can make you stronger. I said it CAN make you stronger, because you either become a winner or a victim (stronger or weaker).

The second one is useless pain. It is suffering. It happens when you decide to stay with that pain, because somehow you feel comfortable with that pain. We are humans, when something hurts us, of course that we will suffer. But for how long, and what you will learn from it, well, that only depends on you.

Life goes on... yet, it only depends on you how pain will change you.

256

"Life is too short to worry about what others say or think about you. Have fun and give them something to talk about"

Ha-ha... people and their perspectives. A never-ending story...

All my life, I've been listening "stories" about myself. Even today people talk about me but I choose not to listen. Why would I? I don't care! If you want to know me, talk to me, not others. And I decide what I will share and with whom.

At the beginning it bothered me, mostly because the stories weren't true, and I don't like injustice! I haven't changed in that aspect, I still dislike injustice, but I did change my perspective, and reaction.

Also, I was thinking, if I don't speak about others, why others speak about me?! Do they have their own life to speak about? Obviously not. That is my perspective! I am a type of person who don't like small talk, chit-chat and stuff.

Then I learnt that it is not about me, but them. How one sees you, it speaks more about them, not you. Mostly, when people have no life, they try to create some drama in yours, talking negatively about you! No, no, no. Not nice. But let them talk, dog barks, elephant walks.

Remember this: What Susie says of Sally says more of Susie than of Sally.

Live and let live!

257

"Young girls need to learn that sexiness isn't about being naked." – Marc Jacobs

Not just young girls, though...

Sexiness has nothing to do with being naked.

What naked means if there's not a bit of mystery?

Sexiness has nothing to do with the clothes you wear. You wear your clothes and not vice versa. Sexiness is not putting tones of makeup to look like millions of other girls/women. Don't forget to put your eyebrows, please.

Sexiness is feeling good in your own skin with or without makeup. Having manners, self-confidence and so many other not so visible things, mixed together, will make you look and feel sexy.

So, please gaaal, put your clothes on, don't show everything to everyone. Self-esteem and self-respect are things you must learn first.

258

"Holiday To-Dos: be present, wrap someone in a hug, send love, donate food, make peace, be the light."

And not just on holidays.

How about this?

How about "worrying" about being present in someone's life and be there for them instead of compensating this with money?

We all love gifts, that's completely fine. I love surprises very much. To surprise and to be surprised.

But let's be more aware of life, our loved ones, friends and not take them for granted.

Sometimes, all we need is someone who will be there. To listen, to give us a hug. And if you think a bit more, there are no gifts who can repay for this.

You know when Christmas is coming, the time of the year when people love each other and spoil each other, but what about the rest of the year? Hmmm?

259

"When I hear somebody say 'Life is hard', I am always tempted to ask 'Compared to what?'" - Sydney J. Harris

The importance of asking ourselves the right questions.

Sometimes, when people talk about their problems, I am like, oh, you really see that as a "PROBLEM"?! I remember very well, once, a friend of mine was stressing out because she broke her nail. She was complaining and crying about that while she was in the hospital visiting me! Maybe this was something that triggered something much deeper within her, but that doesn't matter for this post.

Simply, it was one of those a-ha moments. I've learnt a big lesson in my life. Very often, people are not aware of what they are talking about when they talk about life, happiness, problems. They just complain and they are always worried about something, thinking that their current problem is the biggest one in the whole world. So sometimes I ask them: COMPARED TO WHAT?

It's all about your focus.

They don't think about what they have, taking their life for granted.

At the same time, I was like wooow, if that is your biggest "problem", you're blessed.

We learn about life and people more when we listen and observe. I guarantee you that.

So, the next time you catch yourself thinking about problems, ask yourself this.

260

"If you're not willing to put in the effort, don't expect anything in return."

Lots of people are expecting things from others without giving them anything in return. Some of them go even further by getting angry if you don't fulfil their expectations! For fucks sake?! I mean, seriously? How dare I not to live by expectations you have from me? Naughty me. When was the last time you had your ego checked?

Ego problem. Immaturity. Lack of basic manners.

Show me no respect, and I will show you the way out of my life.

You see, it's as simple as that.

So, my question is: How dare you expect anything without giving? Whether it is respect, kindness, time, responsibility, love, just name it.

Make sure that you possess the values you expect from others. Effort equals results!

Actually, I wouldn't say effort, because this should be something natural. A character trait.

Those who want respect, they SHOW respect.

Those who want loyalty, they ARE loyal.

Got it?

Be a giver!

261

"She distanced herself to save herself."

Life lessons.

Sometimes we must step back and look at the big picture.

To stay quiet. To clear our minds. To recharge our batteries.

To spend time on our own. It is so important to spend time alone. When we distance ourselves, we (might) be surprised with what we can see.

If you are the one who recharges batteries when you spend time alone, then do it. Don't be afraid. Do it and pay attention how people who surround you will react.

If you don't value your time and yourself, then who will? Distance and silence speak more than you think. Only those who care about you will know the reason behind your silence. Only those who care about you will look for you when you distance yourself. They will understand you.

On the other hand, there will be those who will not understand you. At all. Even when you explain your reasons. They may feel angry. Don't let them drain you. If you need to distance yourself to save yourself from them, do it.

You do your reset, re-adjustment. Take time for yourself. To take a breath, to have a rest.

And, pay attention.

262

"Don't get drained trying to play the healer in every relationship."

I've been there, done that, that's not good at all. No, no. No.

Your partner shouldn't be there to entertain you or to be your therapist. Neither should your mother or father.

Your job is to heal yourself, before you start any other relationship.

And your partner should be your partner. Relationship is all about building together. Making each other better.

That's something I had to learn. I was successful healing them, but I was so drained at the same time. I didn't put any limits to it, I didn't know that back then, and as a "consequence", now I have a looong volunteering experience. Maybe I should include it in my CV.

Only now, I charge per session.

It's so important to learn how to set limits and to know the balance. Especially if you are a giver and an empath. Know the difference between making each other better and losing yourself trying to fix others.

Thus, now I can only give you my contact data and account number for €/session.

Seriously.

263

A first-date question: "How aware are you of your traumas & suppressed emotions and tell me about how you are actively working to heal them before you try to project that shit on me."

That's legit!

Steeep back. Don't touch my aura with your dirty hands!

No, really, we all have our past traumas and that's just fine! The thing is what we are doing with them.

So please, before you start bleeding on someone who didn't cut you, heal your traumas first.

Your partner should not be there as your therapist or to entertain you or be your garbage bin.

And stop blaming your ex-partners for everything. Don't go around talking bad about them. Let me remind you, they were your "choices". Oh, I know, some of you will say, yeah, that was a huge mistake. But was it?

First of all, that is your private thing. Secondly, you can talk only from your own perspective.

And speaking bad about your ex won't make you a better person. And you won't feel better either.

So, find the reason why you are no longer together and take responsibility for your actions.

Be mature and responsible, take your time to heal, to learn what did you like and what you didn't about them, what made you feel good, and what didn't.

Otherwise, you will attract the same kind of partners and you will share your traumas with them. And trust me, no one deserves your shit.

Please, stop projecting your shit on others.

264

"I have helped people heal while being completely broken myself"

True story.

Don't be afraid of being broken, don't be afraid to ask for help. Forget about that stupid idea that society gives us that it is wrong to say "out loud" that you feel sad, bad, that you struggle.

You are afraid of being proclaimed crazy. No, you are not crazy. And you shouldn't be ashamed of how you feel. Never!

Don't answer with "I'm fine" if you're not.

Just find those who understand you, with whom you can speak to about everything, surround yourself with similar people and open yourself. And don't forget to be there for them too.

That's why we are here, to help and support each other.

A warrior is not all about perfection, victory or invulnerability. A warrior is all about coping with its ABSOLUTE vulnerability.

That's the ONLY TRUE COURAGE.

So, go on and find that warrior within you!

265

"Keep up your faith to go high and fly, even after so many pains and sorrow. You can turn from a caterpillar to a butterfly. Life gives you a second change: a call to grow." - Ana Claudia Antunes

But there is a catch.

You will grow as a person, only if YOU work on yourself. No one can do that for you.

Learn, challenge your limits, confront your fears, question your beliefs, face with your pain...

Forgive.

Accept and embrace yourself. With all your flows.

You know, prepare yourself to feel comfortable around the uncomfortable. Because sometimes it will be. Painful.

But that's just a process, if you really want to bloom.

266

"Being male is a matter of birth. Being a man is a matter of age. But being a gentleman is a matter of choice." – Vin Diesel

Word.

Yesssss and the same goes for women too!

Manners, good education, respect, integrity, among other things, are something I really look for when I speak to people.

Soooo important to me.

Nowadays, this is so rare to find.

If you want a lady by your side, make sure you are a gentleman first. And vice versa.

As usual, Expectations vs. Offer. They must be on the same level.

267

"No one is more hated than he who speaks the truth." – Plato

Well, we all have our truths and we all live our realities.

BUT, there are also some "universal" truths, situations in life, that people like to skip, hide, lie, even cheat, creating chaos in other people's lives.

I don't like this: No names, no shames.

Why not pointing out when somebody is doing something wrong? By staying silent you are their accomplice. Keep this in mind.

I prefer: The world is a dangerous place, not because of those who do evil, but because of those who look at it and do nothing.

We have all been witnesses to some kind of injustice. Whether we talk about domestic violence, bullying or anything else.

The question is: What was your reaction?

People usually turn their head to the other direction. Don't be one of them. Please.

We all know when we do/see something wrong. We have common sense, right? But, how many people use it?

I will never stop speaking the truth and pointing out to any kind of injustice.

This can be pretty hard, because people don't like to hear the truth, especially when they hide behind a lie.

You may like me or not, none of my business. I would rather be hated for who I am, than to be loved for something I am not!

268

"Apply for that job. Date that person. Buy that plane ticket. Do all the things that scare you, because they're worth it."

I know some of you will say: Easier said than done.

But it doesn't mean that it is impossible.

Where there's a will, there's a way.

Let me tell you something, if fear is the reason that stops you from doing things. be aware that fear is nothing but your thought, which means that you are the one who stops yourself from doing it.

Take a risk, find the way to do something you want to do and just do it. No excuses.

If not today, then tomorrow Hack, whenever possible.

Ask her out, tell him you love him or miss him, book that plane ticket, challenge yourself to do all those things that scare you!

Don't let it sit within you, decide to do it and do it. No matter what.

You can only lose by being indecisive. It is always better to do something and know the result than keep thinking: what if? Should I do it?

You don't lose just because things don't turn out how you've expected.

In this case, there are no wrong or right decisions, just decisions that we make that will bring us new adventures, possibilities, where we will challenge ourselves and who knows what else?

Well, we can only find out after we do it.

269

"It's okay to not be okay"

It is ok to not be ok!

Don't put yourself under the pressure that you have to feel fine if you don't.

Help yourself feel better doing what you love.

Give yourself time to process and heal whatever you are going through.

Suppressing your emotions won't do you any good.

Sometimes instant solutions aren't the best ones.

You just can't turn off feelings and turn on the "happy-smile mode". Don't listen to those who tell you that. Just smile and everything will be fine. No, no, no. Life doesn't work that way. You are not a light switch.

Yet, you can help yourself heal faster.

Take some time for yourself. To readjust, to refuel yourself both mentally and physically. Be alone. Simply, you crave for that inner conversation. To see what is causing those feelings. Things that hurt you. Talk about it. Accept it. Let it go. This might be the hardest part, so give yourself some time to let go of anything/ anyone that make you feel bad. And heal step by step, doing stuff you like. It's a process.

Listen to your inner voice. That is your guidance.

Remember: It's just a bad day, not a bad life!

And do yourself a favour and avoid those who say that is not okay to not be okay. Please.

270

"I was doing ok, then I woke up." – Peanuts

When your dreams are better than your reality...

But, that's one of the purposes of our dreams, to show us that everything is possible. Sometimes you wake up with a solution that you had in your dreams. At least it happened to me.

I'm also a daydreamer.

And never stop dreaming. Every dream can come true. If you work on that. Believing is essential.

271

"Where knowledge ends, religion begins." - Benjamin Disraeli

My humble opinion:

We are all spiritual human beings. It's a fact.

To me there is only one religion and that is love.

When I choose people who surround me, I choose them based on my standards, not based on religion.

And religion... religion has been invented to separate people. The easiest way to start an argue, to hate others, to judge, to start wars!

Why? When we all have our own God, within us, our true self.

Love. Love is something that connects us all. Not religion, but love.

If you need to judge others, judge them for who they are, not for their religion.

Listen to you heart! Have faith and believe in your God – yourself.

And if you are a religious person, pleeeeease respect other cultures and religions the same way you would like them to respect your choice.

Those who want respect, they give respect.

Peace and LOVE.

272

"Fill your life with experiences, not thing. Have stories to tell, not stuff to show."

I know... we live in a world where people are becoming so materialistic and selfish, and most of them think that money can bring happiness. Don't get me wrong, money is important, but not for happiness. Money serves to make this life easier. Thus, it is very important.

But happiness is a state of mind. A kind of decision, if you ask me.

What you're looking for is that feeling of excitement when you buy a new pair of shoes or any other thing you love.

But what happens after a couple of days? You still have the same pair of shoes, but that feeling of excitement disappeared.

And what do you do/think? You think that you need to buy something new and that's why you think that money buys and brings happiness.

The fact is that you don't need a new pair of shoes, but what you actually look for is that feeling you have when you buy something you like.

Happiness is nothing but a result of the inner job. Do whatever makes you feel good, whatever nurtures your soul, whatever sparkles your life, and trust me, the less thing you need, the happier you will become.

273

"There is no exquisite beauty... without some strangeness in the proportion." - Edgar Allan Poe

Without some uniqueness. As a matter of fact, we are all unique, yet we live in a world where people behave like robots trying to copy others and look like each other.

It is really, reeeally rare to find real, natural, genuine beauty that shines inside out.

We live in a world with superficial values, in which people compare themselves to others, watching their photos on Instagram or any other social media. They try to look like someone else, dress like others, following their rituals, diets etc., mostly for all the wrong reasons.

And so many of them have forgotten to work on themselves. From the inside. To nurture their souls, minds, hearts, all of which should be in alignment.

Our inner beauty will never age, but our bodies will.

Accept and embrace yourself as you are, learn to love your body and to be kind to yourself. This should be your starting point. Then, work on yourself to be better inside and outside. Your goal should be to feel happy and healthy from within. And to live a fulfilled life, instead of putting pressure on yourself following others and trying to live their lives. You are you, not them.

Yo', boys and gals, you weren't born to look like somebody else.

274

"Your scars are beautiful just like you."

No... your scars are not beautiful just like you. Your scars are You, and You are beautiful just the way you are. They are a part of you! Within you or on your skin, either way, they are you, your story!

We all have scars.

You shouldn't be ashamed of them. They remind you that you are brave and they tell story about how you got over something and how you became stronger.

Some of us, we have scars on our bodies too. I have a plenty of them (due to the accident and many non-cosmetic surgeries). That's something I had to learn to accept. Sometimes, I thought it was more difficult to overcome them than those within, because we live in a world where people judge you based on your appearance. But not only because of that, but also because you have to accept the fact that your body is not the same anymore.

If you know people who make you feel less worthy because of your scars, or those who judge you and value you based on something that hurt you, they need to go away from your life. Immediately.

Make sure you don't start valuing yourself through the eyes of others, especially those who don't see your worth and those who don't respect your life story!

I love to say: Fuck the people with no scars, they have no story to tell. And fuck those who don't respect your story!

275

"I'm selfish, impatient and a little insecure. I make mistakes, I am out of control and at times hard to handle. But if you can't handle me at my worst, then you sure as hell don't deserve me at my best." – Marilyn Monroe

If you can't stick with me in "my bad times" then for sure you don't deserve me at my best! I was always saying this.

If we try to think that bad or good times actually don't exist, let's say it is all just life and its different situations. And what matters is how you handle them. Some of you will say and what if you lose someone, that's horrible. Like I said, that is all life. But that's another story.

So, if someone decides not to stay with you just because life doesn't go smoothly as he/she expected, then he/she is doing you a favour. Yes, it hurts, but you don't need them. You need support. It is all about expectations here. Your reasonable expectation is that the one who is by your side will stick with you, supporting you in all life situations. The same way you would do for them (hopefully). And that person has different expectations from any kind of relationship.

This also speaks a lot about themselves. If you and your life are intimidating to them, it only speaks about your strength and their weakness. You need someone of your level to face this life together with you, not some immature person. They need to grow, and you need love.

And VICE VERSA, as usual.

276

"Be the reason someone smiles today."

Be a giver!

Everything you do or give will come back to you in some unexpected ways.

If every single one of us do something nice for someone and put the smile on their face... we would have the world full of smiles. And that's something we need!

Whatever it is, a kind word, a hug, a joke or a nice message, please do it.

May this day bring you peace, tranquillity and harmony.

277

"Eat whatever you want and if anyone tries to lecture you about your weight eat them too!"

Eat them too!

It's a lack of basic manners when someone looks at your plate and counts your bites!

We are all different and we have different needs. Depending on so many factors.

Nutrition is so important for our overall wellbeing and health.

But...

When you crave for some food, comfort food, the last thing you need is someone trying to lecture you about health. Like that's something you don't already know.

So eat them too!

Health is not just eating healthy food, but also having a smile on your face. Chocolate can do that without asking any unnecessary questions.

If you eat that extra slice of pie, or maybe the entire pie or cookies, a pizza for 4, if you crave it – eat it! You won't eat like that every day.

Restricting yourself can develop a bad relationship with food. And in the long run, it won't be good for you.

Listening to others can also develop the feeling of guilt and you really don't need that, especially not after enjoying the food.

Enjoy your life and live your life happily and healthily.

Disclaimer: I'm not encouraging you to eat more than you need, you know the best how much you need. I'm just saying that your body knows what it needs so listen to it instead of listening to other people.

278

"Judge me by the people I avoid."

Tell Me Your Friends And I Will Tell You Your Future.

279

"Stronger together."

We are all one!

When you fill your heart with love, everything seems different.

Different on so many levels.

Instead of judging, try to understand.

Respect the differences, different cultures, different skin colours, heights, weights. In the end, we are all the same! We are all one, yet so different. Same spirits in different physical bodies.

Without the love in your heart, I'm afraid none of this is possible for you to see.

We are not here to judge, but to support each other.

Where there is a judgment there is no love.

And who are we to judge one another?

One needs to see with one's heart to be able to understand.

Mind can fool you, but your heart never will.

Namaste!

Love & peace!

280

"Be a lotus flower. Be in the water, and do not let the water touch you." – Osho

Yet it is very challenging to stay calm when you're tormented.

But that's the point! I think I can't stress this enough.

If you wish one calm, peaceful life, this should be your objective and you should be working on it. On your inner peace.

Clear your mind by taking some time, because you can't see your reflection in the boiling water.

Everything comes from within! It's not about life but you, and how you react to it.

And those reactions will shape your personality, your decisions, which will determine your future!

If you keep worrying, complaining, and you feel good about it, then, great, keep doing it. I will give you all my problems to worry about them too. And let me know if you find a solution, just by worrying about them.

281

"He doesn't lie to you because the truth will hurt your feelings. He lies to you because the truth might provoke you to make choices that won't serve his interests."

One of those things I dislike is when someone assumes things that have nothing to do with me. Oh, boy... And in this case, if someone decides not to tell me something, assuming that may hurt me...

Oh, pardon my French, but that's complete and utter bullshit.

You are not doing this to protect me or others, but to protect yourself! You don't want to be that "bad cop" because you fear that they will change their opinion about you. Thus, you have a couple of issues:

1. You care what others will think of you.

2. People who "love you" don't love the real you, but the image of you that you have created.

3. You are not loyal to them but to your need for them.

Think from the opposite perspective!

If someone lies to you or if you lie to someone, that's an act of egoism and irresponsibility, and it shows a lack of respect. As a result, you can create more problems than you can imagine.

The truth, no matter how hard it is, has to be told. Yes, it's not going to be easy to say/listen to it, but find the way to do it. And help them deal with the truth. Or would you rather live in a lie?

Be responsible, your actions speak about you! So, if you are lying... what does it say about you?

Truth, trust and respect above all.

282

"I have learned to love the sky because it's always there. And learned to unlove the people who were not."

You don't have to unlove them!

You can love them, and wishing them all the best but if they are not good for you, you can simply choose to let them go.

Yes, you can love someone from the distance.

Also, if you want to "unlove" someone just because it's not always there, it's selfish. Maybe that someone also needs you to understand them, maybe they can't be there for you this time, but the next time they would.

So before you "unlove" someone, make sure that you are doing it for the right reasons. Communication, like always, is the key. Speaking and expressing how you feel is so important.

283

"A head full of fears has no room for dreams."

Fear is the product of your thoughts, let's not confuse it with any real danger.

Danger is real. But it doesn't mean that something will happen.

And 99% of things you fear or you worry about, will never happen. But you will put your body under the same level of stress like it will. You will live it just by thinking about it.

The same way when you think about nice things, and thus switch your body to the relax mode.

Try this exercise. First you have to be aware of your thoughts, then when you start to fill your head with negative thoughts, try to replace them with some positive thoughts. Intentionally, you have to break that circle of negative thoughts, because they will lead you to overthinking, anxiety, stress etc.

Your mind is a very powerful tool!

Rule your mind or let your mind rule you!

You decide!

284

"You are worth more than second thoughts and maybes."

If you are indecisive:

Do not think too much if you want to do something, it's the maybes that will destroy you.

We all think 24/7, unless you've learnt how to shut off your brain.

Thus, pick your thoughts wisely. Thoughts that will serve you. Your mind is a powerful tool. Either you will learn how to rule your mind or you will let your mind rule you.

Listen to your heart, it knows the way.

If your heart says yes, then do it. Decide and stick to your decision.

No matter the fear, the what-ifs, those are just your thoughts stopping you from doing things.

And if someone is indecisive about you, sending you mixed signals and confused feeling, let them go. They need to deal with that, not you. You are worth so much more than being an option for someone. You deserve someone who knows that they want you.

And vice versa.

285

"How he treats you is how he feels about you. Don't try to decode it or make excuses, it's simple. If he acts like he doesn't care, he doesn't care!"

Don't try to paint a new picture or to find excuses for someone's behaviour (they are busy, stressed etc.), just because you wish that badly. Just because you care. Just because you wish that they care too.

No, darling, if they act like they don't care, they don't care.

And you don't need that.

You need someone who cares! Someone who won't make excuses, who will treat you right, the way you deserve.

How they treat you is how they feel about you. Believe them.

It's as simple as that.

Be with someone who will take care of you. not materialistically, but take care of your soul, your well being, your heart.

286

"The great pleasure in life is doing what people say you cannot do." – Walter Bagehot

I am not sure whether it is the greatest pleasure or not, but the pleasure is definitely immense!

It's like a win-win situation, and we love win-win situations, right?

People usually say that you can't do something just because they are not capable of doing it. Don't let them stop you.

I had a couple of situations in my life and I didn't let them stop me follow my intuition and I didn't allow that their limits and opinions become my reality.

If you think you can, you're right.

Remember you are doing that for yourself! Not for them, or because of them. Believe in yourself and use them like a nitro to boost yourself, but do it for yourself!

287

"Babe can you let down your emotional walls?"

"You're asking something very difficult of me."

"I can help, we can start with small steps..."

Let's say that we all have some kind of "trauma" from past relationships. Any kind of relationship. Or from dealing with people in general.

If you like someone and you would love them to be part of your life, don't expect them to behave like you would like them to behave. Don't push them to open themselves, instead try to accept them as they are. Try to understand their way of thinking/behaving and try to be supportive.

Let them feel safe with you and you would be surprised how easily will things flow.

The more you push things, the less they will flow.

Treat others the same way you would like to be treated.

288

"You are loved. You are needed. You make this world so much more beautiful just by being in it."

Yes, you are.

Isn't it beautiful and powerful that the world wouldn't be the same without you? Without any of us? We are all connected somehow. And we all have changed, we change and we will change each other's life.

Let's try to have an influence, always for the better.

If you can't make someone's life better, you should remove yourself from their lives.

It's all about choices.

Making someone else's life better will make your life better.

How powerful is that? When you have one of those days, remind yourself that this world needs you!

289

"Seeing unhealthy patterns in your family and deciding that those patterns end with you and will not be passed down to future generations, is an extremely brave & powerful decision."

And we all have that power!

We all have common sense, but not all of us are using it.

We have all been raised without being asked whether something was wrong or not. We simply had to accept it, because we didn't have another option. So we adopted our parents' beliefs, standards and perspectives as something normal.

People usually point fingers at other families, judging them or commenting: they aren't normal. They would rarely point finger at themselves, asking themselves whether the teaching they pass on their kids is normal or not? Are they good parents?

Ok, as kids I'm sure that all of us have experienced some kind of "injustice", thinking & saying: "Oh, I can't wait to grow up to start living on my own", or "I will never be like you", etc.

Sounds familiar?

There is rarely anyone who remembers this when they finally grow up. There is rarely anyone who abandons the adopted unhealthy patterns.

You know, it's not your fault if you have been being raised in some unhealthy conditions. But it is your responsibility to abandon the unhealthy patterns in your family. There's so many ways to do it, but they all require growing some balls.

Be brave, for you, your kids and for future generations!

Start by a simple thing, by questioning things and beliefs. We all have the ability to distinguish right from wrong.

290

"You can't make someone be ready for what you're ready for, and you're not obligated to wait around for them to make up their mind."

In the same way you can't heal or help others, if they don't want to be helped.

Don't wait for those who might never come.

Don't settle for anybody who leaves you wondering.

Don't prioritise those who treat you like an option.

Don't wait for those who leave you with mixed feelings, just because they are insecure in their own.

And vice versa, don't expect others to be there for you if you... – everything from the list above applies.

Some great *don'ts* and *can'ts* can save your time and energy. Learn the difference between those with whom you waste your time and those who deserve your patience.

Essential.

291

"At this age, I'm no longer explaining basic principles of respect and loyalty. Either you show me you already know, or I'm falling back, no in between."

Neither should you try to teach others how to behave. That's something we learn from our parents.

But we can re-teach others by giving them an example.

If they see they were wrong, I guess that was a lesson they have to learn. It's up to them whether they will apply what they've learnt or not.

And we all change. Some people for the better, and then some...

it seems like they never change. It's all up to us, and our choices, the decisions we make.

The same way you can't force someone to respect you, that's their choice. But you can refuse to be disrespected. That can be your choice.

Remember, those who want respect, they give respect. Those who want loyalty, ARE loyal.

Show me a lack of respect and I'll show you the door. And I'll be so kind to hold the door for you, on your way out. Because, you know, I have manners.

292

"Support your friends' businesses and progressions like you support the celebrities that you don't actually know."

Ha-ha, love this quote.

Seeing people supporting each other is so rare nowadays.

How come it is easier to support celebrities than your friend?

Simply because you think that somehow you will be "jeopardized" if your friend succeeds and you don't (whatever success means to you). They will remind you that you could do something, but you didn't.

The thing is that you are just too lazy or full of fears and insecurities to move your ass and change your life. And if your friend fails you will use it as an excuse to justify yourself to you. But, you will know the truth deep inside.

And a celebrity is already famous and not a part of your life.

Generally, people will SAY they support you, but is that really what they think? Don't trust their words, but their energy.

We live in a competitive world where people compare their lives with other people's lives. God forbid that you're doing better than them...

If you fail, as I said, they will feel better about themselves and they will feel relief, giving you words of support at the same time.

Pay attention...

Behind all that lie different types of fear and insecurities! Insecurities converted into jealousy, envy, gossip.

The most important thing: I hope that you are not one of those people who feel "happy" when other people fail.

293

"Do online relationships work out? Can you actually fall in love?"

Oh, those virtual connections, internet and long-distance relationships...

Are they real? Or Instant? A quick escape from reality? Lonely hearts? Lonely hearts in relationships/marriages?

Whatever the circumstances, I hope they will find "real love and real relationship". I truly wish and hope so. You know I live for love and I love when love wins. True love.

Are you familiar with this? I'm sure you are. I'm sure, I think we have all experienced this...

294

"You remind me of a no thanks."

You know those people you meet and you realize you want to spend the rest of your day, days, life without them?

Yes, I know them too.

I understand some people live in their own little world. I have my own little world too, and sometimes I wish they would stay there and never visit mine.

Sorry, not sorry.

Your energy introduces you before you say a word. Energy never lies.

295

"People don't care for you when you are alone, they just care for you when they are alone."

Actually, not because they are alone, but rather lonely.

Spending time alone can be very beneficial.

On the other hand, many lonely people on the planet are looking for others to make them feel better.

So many of them are lonely although they are in a relationship.

If you're expecting others to make you feel happy, that's a really wrong way to feel better. Your partner is not there to entertain you. If you need entertainment, maybe you should try going to the circus.

Know that all you look for is already within you. Not in others, but within you.

No one can make you happy, but you.

Buying a new pair of shoes or a new car won't make you happy, other people won't make you happy, partners won't make you happy. You should have all these in your life because you love them not because you need them to make you feel happy.

Apart from this, know that very few people genuinely care how you feel. And those are keepers.

Learn the difference. And love yourself. That way you will never feel lonely.

296

"I'm not inspired by people who act inspiring. I'm inspired by people who are brutally honest with themselves."

Me, I'm not a fan of people who act like they know what they are talking about. Way too many of them. Motivational copy/paste speakers. No, no, no.

Or those who put their name under someone else's quote. Why would you do that?

I have my own theory. If I say something and find out later that someone already said that, me happy! Please remind me of the age of the earth? Everything we say, think, speak, someone else has probably already said it! And I'm happy I had to understand something and figure it out on my own.

There is a huge difference between genuine revelations and the copy/paste approach.

Naturally, I'm a huuuuge fan of people whose lives inspire me. Those who hit the rock bottom before climbing to the top. I'm a fan of people's real experiences and of those I can learn from. Fan of people who walk the talk. Of raw intelligence. Of those who have stories to tell, who know how to speak, to explain themselves, who use their words impeccably when they express themselves. Simple words. Simple people. It's all about simplicity.

No time to waste here on some blah blah blah talk.

297

"You can't heal if you don't feel."

The importance of healing... If you want one calm life and peace from within... you have to (learn how to) feel and how to deal with situations.

There is no other way around!

Simply, if you look for a rainbow, you have to know there was a storm before.

Suppressing or escaping from your feelings won't make you feel better. On the contrary.

My dear, the one who broke you or some situation that broke you can't heal you. I wish they could.

What stops you from having a better life? Nothing, but you!

And the fear of fear.

Fear of any judgment if you admit that you're feeling hurt.

Fear of pain. But aren't you already living in pain? Do you feel that you suffer from some unhealed wounds? You don't have to. It's your choice.

298

"If my absence doesn't affect your life then my presence has no meaning in it."

Sooo true...

If my absence doesn't affect you, then there must be something wrong with you!

Jooooking. Or not. Anyway...

I would kindly and gently remove myself from lives of those who don't appreciate my presence.

299

"The most beautiful people I think in this world are the ones that have that unique courage to be themselves. No matter what anyone says, no matter how many people laugh or mock them, they continue to be themselves even if they are alone. They don't change to get anyone like them. They smile because they're happy and content with themselves."

It really takes true courage and strength to follow your own heart and live the life according to your standards. To be free. To feel free.

That's what self-confidence and strength are.

Way toooo many people live up to other people's expectations, without being aware of it. They SAY oh, I don't care what people think of me. BUT their reality is completely different.

That's why you should question everything. Your beliefs, your actions, because we are all programmed and brainwashed since the day 1.

You were born free. Don't imprison yourself.

I smile. Not because my life is perfect and I have no problems, actually I have some real struggles at this point of my life. I smile because I'm so happy with who I am.

I really don't care what others think about me. I mean, I REALLY and truly don't care. I learned that lesson a long time ago. I don't depend on other people's opinions and I don't see myself through other people's eyes.

So...

I smile. And I hope, my reader, you're smiling too.

300

"Do not allow your loneliness to lower your standards. Read that again."

And read it again...

You receive what you give. In case you don't like your current situation, whether we talk about love, job or life in general, ask yourself why you settle down if you think you deserve more?

Speaking about relationships: oh boy, I will try to keep it short.

Do you love yourself? If you do, I'm sure you know what feels good for your heart, body and mind.

You should never settle down for anything less than you deserve. You shouldn't lower your standards because you are afraid to be alone. You shouldn't pretend that you are with the right one for you when you're not, simply because if you love yourself, you should be honest to yourself.

You should not allow your loneliness lower your standards,

finding all possible excuses to justify yourself for being with someone who doesn't feel right.

I often see people with standards high as the size of heels I wear. And I wear no heels.

Self-love is a must. You won't feel lonely. Even when a day comes that makes you feel lonely a bit, you know, the time when you could use a hug or two, even then you will know that it is better to hug a teddy bear and stay single, than to be in a relationship and feel miserable.

301

"Every time I lower my frequency to meet someone on their level I end up paying for it. That's a lesson I really don't need to learn anymore. Rise up to meet me."

Call it whatever you like: standards, frequency, vibration, it doesn't matter. If you are not in alignment with yourself, the result will be the same until you change something.

That's the lesson I don't need to repeat anymore.

I refuse to shrink myself so other can feel comfortable in my surroundings.

Shrinking myself has brought me nothing good, instead I constantly felt misunderstood.

Exhausted of trying to explain myself to people who simply couldn't understand me. And that's the only thing I wanted, to be understood and accepted from people I love(d).

Back then, I didn't know this.

Now, I do.

I can't change them neither should I, no matter my good intentions. No matter my love.

But I changed. I no longer shrink myself for someone else's comfort!

And that thing, that change of mindset, my beautiful souls, that thing wasn't easy, but sooo worth it. Priceless.

Now I feel free.

302

"I don't live in darkness. Darkness lives in me."

I really don't know why people try to neglect the existence of their dark side.

The fact is that WE ALL have a good and a "bad" side. Or a positive and a negative side of us. Good and bad thoughts.

What's the point of neglecting the fact then?

But which part of us will be dominant, you guess, depends on us.

We will never get rid of negative thoughts. Our bad feelings, fears, behaviours, habits, all these together create our dark side. Don't even try to ignore them.

There is also that positive bright side of us. Pure love, joy, motivation, positive thoughts and self-talk, kindness, affirmative behaviours, habits and emotions that make our lives better and brighter.

First and foremost, you should be aware of them. To accept yourself the way you are.

And then, whichever side you nurture more, will win.

If you let yourself be controlled by frustrations, anger etc., your dark side will win. This is usually coming from your mind.

Or if you try to forgive, to love, to share, to be kind. This is usually coming from your heart.

We can transform negative energy to the positive one by trying to understand why and where it comes from.

It's up to us! I love Shakespeare's quote: "Hell is empty and all the devils are here".

Don't be afraid to look within, sometimes the worst place you can be is your own head.

303

"Letting toxic people go is not an act of cruelty. It's an act of self-care."

Self-love! Self-care! Self-respect!

None of these have nothing to do with selfishness.

If you believe that you are selfish or you think about what others will think of you, if you can't let go of toxic people, then you should ask yourself:

1. Who taught you that you should accept toxicity as a part of your life and why?

2. Does that belief of accepting toxicity serves you (do you feel good or happy about it)?

3. Are you tolerating it just because someone taught you that you should accept it?

Letting go of anyone who is toxic for you can only be beneficial for you. Whether it is a friend, partner or a family member.

There we go…

304

"If you have a problem with me, call me. If you don't have my number, then that means you don't know me well enough to have a problem." – Eleanor Calder

Ta-daaah.

You don't like me. But how come, if you don't know me!

I really don't mind whether you like me or not (something or everything about me), just remember that judging others, it speaks a lot about you. And, I know I'm loveable.

When you point one finger at someone, there are three fingers pointing back to you!

Know that if you don't like someone and you judge them, there are others who will love everything about them, even those very things you don't like about them.

At the end of the day, here's the moral of the story: when you find yourself triggered by behaviour of a person who has done nothing wrong to you personally, or someone you don't know, you should ask yourself why did it happen?

Know that what we see in others reflects ourselves. That's why we should try to understand why we dislike something about someone?

People are like a mirror to us.

And if you have a problem with me, please call me. Don't talk to others, but to me. So, call me.

“One man’s I’m not ready is another man’s I knew the second I saw her.”

Ladies if he wants you, he’ll move mountains to be with you.

You want that.

Ladies and gentlemen...

You don’t want mixed signals. Neither to give, nor to receive. You don’t want those who don’t know what they want. Simply, because you shouldn’t be an option. The same way you shouldn’t look at the other person like an option.

So...

Never push someone who “is not ready” even though they seem to be good for you. No, they are not. Behind that “I’m not ready”, you have a million reasons why this person doesn’t want to be with you.

Wait for that special one “I knew the second I saw her/him”.

Wait for that one who is not afraid to show how much they care.

Anyway, when is the perfect time to be ready? How do you know that you are ready? Well, you will know it the second you see that person.

You see the difference? Good.

And of course, it goes vice versa.

Simply, don’t play with other people’s emotions if you are not sure in your own feelings. If your intentions are not serious enough.

Playing with another person's emotions is an act of cowardness.

306

"Stop adding people to your life with the same negative traits as the ones you worked so hard to remove."

Read this again.

Stop wasting your energy and time on same things, situations and people who drained you!

Because...

The same people, situations will repeat in your life until you learn the lesson.

Have you ever wondered why do you meet similar type of people repeatedly? You know, have you ever caught yourself saying this: but you are exactly the same as my ex (or any other person)? I did.

Or do you tend to go back to your ex even though that was a toxic environment for you?

Or you stay in a relationship that doesn't feel right for you?

Stop it. It's your choice.

You can't expect things to change if you always do the same things. It's not about others, but you.

I know, I know, mind blowing, but please read it again.

307

"Stop chasing people... If they block you, cut off contact with you, or ignore you... let them go. Let the people who naturally gravitate to you enjoy your energy. We spend so much time begging people to stay, "proving our worth", clinging to them so that they won't have room to leave. Cherish the people who WANT to talk to you, who WANT to see you, who are there by CHOICE, and not there because you chased them every time they decided to bail on you" – Dru Edmund Kucherera

Another stop-doing thing... (of course only if it resonates with you)

Stop chasing people!

Why would you want them to stay in your life if they don't want that? Even worse, if they escape, if they block you or ignore you, actions speak louder than words.

Would you like that someone chases you after you said them that you no longer want to be part of their life?

So., why?

Don't even run to catch a bus. The next one will come.

So why would you run after someone?

People come and go. But your self-respect should always stay with you. The same way the right people will stay.

Wish them all the best and let them go.

And focus on yourself, people who appreciate you and your presence.

Who check up on you because they care for you, not because they need you.

308

"It matters not who you love, where you love, why you love, when you love, or how you love. It matters only that you love." – John Lennon

Love! Be love, give love and share love! The world needs more love!

But first and foremost, love yourself first, because if we speak about partners, yes, IT MATTERS who you love.

Other than that. Just love!

309

"She let it go. She was ready to vibrate higher and become a magnet to miracles. Now she is in this place where everything feels right. Her heart is calm. Her soul is lit. Her vision is clear. She's at peace with where she's been. And at peace with where she's headed."

Maybe not everything feels right from the outside, and it never will because you can't control life, but from within, hell yes, it can feel right.

That's the only thing that matters! Your inner peace.

Thus, it's so important to let go of anything that holds you back and distracts you from keeping your heart calm.

Make peace with your past.

Forgive.

Forgiving doesn't mean approving. But understanding why something happened.

Forgive people, but firstly, forgive yourself whenever you weren't kind to yourself and move on keeping in mind that your inner peace should be your number one priority.

310

"Don't let your loyalty become slavery. Know when to let go, never compromise on self-respect."

It's always a great time for self-analysis. Says no one ever.

Jokes aside, it's very important to constantly question your beliefs, habits, ideas, whether something serves us or not. If it doesn't, we should change it.

Change is not an easy process, but it's the right thing to do.

If you are a loyal person, cherish that, because that's beautiful and very rare to see nowadays. We need more people with integrity.

But don't stay loyal to someone or something that shows no reciprocity in it or doesn't make you feel good, doesn't respect you or takes advantage of you. These people take you for granted.

You allowed that. Because you didn't respect yourself in the first place by choosing to be loyal to those who don't appreciate it. You have forgotten to be loyal to yourself.

And that's normal. We always view situations from our perspectives, thinking that people will respect us the same way we respect them.

It doesn't mean that you should start being disloyal. It means that you should let go of those who don't appreciate you.

Your loyalty shouldn't be your slavery. A loyal person should be respected. We live in the world where people are usually only loyal to their needs of you, not to you. They don't even know what loyalty means.

Start respecting yourself by being loyal to you and to your inner peace.

311

"Today, enjoy life little moments."

Today and every day! Find at least 10 minutes for yourself and do whatever will nurture your body, mind and soul.

312

"I am not what you think I am. You are what you think I am."

First and foremost, how people see you shouldn't be your business.

You can't change how people see you or feel about you and don't even try.

Focus on yourself instead, on your life. To learn, to grow, to share, strive to become a better person in every possible aspect.

Do good to yourself and to others.

Focus on your relationships with people near and dear to your heart and be humble and kind. First of all, to yourself.

Do things that make you feel good and surround yourself with people who make you feel happy. Be that person for them too.

Be yourself and the right people will stick by your side.

I hope you now have a better understanding about why you shouldn't care what other people think of you. People see you and perceive you from their own perspectives. Perspectives are very different and they depend on so many things.

We are like a mirror to them the same way they are like a mirror to ourselves.

And if you care what others think of you, you put the key to your happiness in their hands.

We are all born free, why would you choose to live like a slave?

313

"Todd: 'Oh great, of course! Here it comes! You can't keep doing this! You can't keep doing shitty things and then feel bad about yourself like that makes it okay! You need to be better!'"

People very often play their victim roles.

But…

Know that you can make a mistake once, but if you keep repeating the same thing over and over again, IT'S YOUR CHOICE!

If you apologize for doing something wrong, but you don't change your behaviour, again, that's your choice.

Can you imagine how mentally exhausting it is for others who trusted you, but you broke their trust? If they leave you, maybe you will finally learn the lesson and take some responsibility for your life.

You lose your credibility and respect like this and people stop trusting you. And how do you feel about that?

No one can change others unless they want to change. If they don't respect you, you can choose to respect yourself and leave them. If you don't leave, that's also your choice, but don't blame them in case they repeat the same thing. You allowed that.

There is always a choice.

Way too many people rather blame everything and everyone else, creating dramas, pitting themselves rather than to TAKE RESPONSIBILITY for their actions, choices etc. and change their behaviour for the better.

Stay away from me, don't touch my aura with your dirty hands.

314

"Stop being available for people who don't prioritize you and your time." - Bryant McGill

Self-respect – one got to learn what self-respect is.

Be there for others, but don't forget to be there for yourself too!

Don't prioritize those who treat you like an option! We all choose our priorities and how we will spend our time.

Know your limits, because people usually don't know your limits and they treat you the way you allow yourself to be treated!

So, if you allow them to treat you like an option, they will!

315

"To love a person is to see all of their magic, and to remind them of it when they have forgotten."

If we would all do this to just one single person every single day, can you even imagine that love energy spreading all around the world?

And, yes, it is possible.

Being kind and nice doesn't cost a thing.

It's your time you spent, energy you shared, and it has a HUGE value.

The same way you will need that someone who will remind you of how magical you are,as we all have ups and downs.

And imagine that impact and change in the world that we (could) make. Yes, we can all do that, together.

The question is: do you (want to) do that?

Love is all we need.

316

"Don't let others influence your thoughts."

"If you don't read the newspaper, you're uninformed. If you read the newspaper, you're mis-informed."

I don't watch TV or read newspapers for more than 10 years. Which means that I'm completely uninformed and I don't regret it not even for a second.

I choose what I will watch and when. I don't want to watch things that others want us to watch and " the truth" they serve to people.

Media serve as an instrument for manipulation. And me, I don't like to be manipulated.

No realities, no politics, no news, no soaps operas.

Simply, that's my decision. If you feel well watching any of these, then keep watching it, congrats. Me, I don't have a stomach for that. So, yes, I'm completely uninformed.

"Don't trust people who tell you other people's secrets."
– Dan Howell

Let me tell you a secret, but please don't tell anyone: I even heard Morgan's voice while I was reading this sentence.

Anyway, know that you are not special to those who tell you other people's secret. Or lie about others.

They will also tell your secrets to others.

That's the way they are.

Don't fool yourself thinking they see you as a good friend they can confess to. They are just, and here I'll try to be nice, they are just people who like to gossip, no-lifers, trying to complicate other people's lives. Cunts.

Consciously or not, they can create a mess in other people's lives. They are miserable so that's the only thing they can share: misery. If they would be full of love, they would be sharing love instead.

Simply, you give what you have.

But they forget that their life can be destroyed with one simple truth.

So, please, understand this and stay away from them.

In case that you are the one who is doing this, stop hurting others and focus on your life asking yourself this: What hurts you deep within, making you think that you are going to feel better by hurting others? Heal that shit from within instead of sharing it around.

it's never too late and you're never too old to change your life.

318

"Yeah, they should've treated you better. They should've cared more. But they didn't and they don't, and your life keeps moving forward."

Yeah, they should've, but they didn't.

It happens. ALL. THE. TIME.

To you, to me, to anybody.

Maybe you should've treated someone else better? How about that? It happens too.

And?

Either way, life goes on. So you can sit down and complain about it, or you can be kind to yourself knowing that you deserve better, trying not to waste your time suffering. Let them go.

Accept the things/people as they are.

Apologize if you are wrong, forgive those who hurt you...

And for cookies sake, keep moving forward.

319

"It's ok to be brave, it's ok to leave."

Be brave to let go of anything that makes you feel unhappy, unwanted, I repeat, ANYTHING! Don't force things, if something doesn't flow, if something doesn't feel right, let it go.

Friends, partners, relationships, food you don't like, city, books, ANYTHING.

Sometimes it's not easy, BUT comparing to what? Forcing "loyalty" to something that doesn't make you feel good is easier than a change?

IT IS OK to leave if things have started to be toxic for you. It takes true courage to leave, but necessary. For you, for your health. And yes, you are brave and strong enough to leave.

YOU, yes YOU, who read this, you deserve to be healthy and happy! The change starts with you! And you are strong enough to change things for the better.

You can thank me later...

320

"I'm not the same soul I once was. A lot has changed. So, you shouldn't expect out of me what I exhibited in the past. For that part of me no longer exists."

I am the same soul, but I've changed!

I put back my pieces differently. Not overnight. Not easy.

But so worth it.

And I will keep chaning. Growing. To always be wiser, stronger, better. For myself and for the world.

And more beautiful, of course.

How about you?

321

"Learn to differentiate between the sound of your intuition guiding you and your traumas misleading you."

Let's face facts: we all have "traumas".

I know, I know, mind blowing.

I don't like the word trauma or making them all so general because bad experiences can be very different.

But what makes a huge difference is the impact of traumas on our lives and how we deal with them and understand them.

For instance, someone hurt you by lying to you. That's a kind of "trauma" for some.

Some people will stop trusting others thinking they will protect themselves that way. Sorry guys, but that's not how life works. That's just your mind telling you to close your heart.

When you close your heart, you will start to lose connection with your intuition, or simply you will ignore it. You will think you're becoming a robot.

Some people will keep trusting others, but they will be more careful about it.

Some people will keep trusting others equally, no matter the past experiences, and they will be hurt over & over again.

Don't close your heart, but learn from your "traumas". Some situations or people we meet will keep repeating and you will think they are all the same, and that's why it is so important to face your "traumas".

322

"Starting over isn't crazy. Crazy is being miserable and walking around half asleep, numb, day after day after day. Crazy is pretending to be happy." - Walter Black - The Beaver (2011)

I'm surprised how many people actually enjoy their unhappiness.

They will try to convince others how happy they are. Actually, they will convince themselves, so they don't have to leave their "comfort zone", because change requires feeling uncomfortable. And to feel comfortable about being uncomfortable requires some guts, which very few people have. As far as I can see.

They will pretend that they are happy, even though they are emotionally 'done', mentally drained, spiritually 'gone'. And when someone asks them how they are, they will smile & say they are fine.

They will continue saying they are great, posting photos of perfect lives, relationships etc., trying to impress others, creating some false image of them & their lives.

But why? Oh, why?

It's NEVER too late to start all over again, regardless your age, current situation or whatever reason you might have.

It won't be easy, you can't expect change to happen overnight or in just one month if you lived your life unfulfilled for who knows how long. So, take your time.

Making one decision is already a start, of course, only if you stick to that decision. Decisions won't work by themselves, unless you do.

Then, make one step at a time.

323

"Stay away from people who make you feel like you're asking for too much when you're demanding what you truly deserve."

You are not asking for too much if you give the same.

If you ask too much, but you do not give the same, well, you know, that's not right. You can't expect loyalty if you are not giving the same. I mean, of course you can expect and ask for it no matter you being disloyal, but hey, that's not nice, you know? That's just being an asshole.

If you know that you give a lot but receive almost nothing, then maybe you should consider leaving or changing something. Whether we talk about jobs, relationships, friendships.

If we talk about expectations, we all have them, but make sure you provide as much as you expect. It's all about expectations vs offer.

Consider this: if someone is telling you that you're asking too much, they either give too little or you're asking too much and not giving enough.

324

"When you don't keep your word, you lose value and credibility."

And trust, and so many other things.

You know if you can't keep your word, then keep your mouth shut.

And apologize if you promised something to someone. They are waiting for you and they trust you, so think about this.

How would you you feel if someone promised you something and they didn't keep their word? Now you see.

Don't be all mouth and no trousers. Please. Think before you speak. It's that simple.

325

"Find someone who knows how to calm your storms." – Donna Aradini

After a storm comes a calm.

We all go through storms, so look for those who know how to help and support you. Simply, those who will make your life easier.

Look for those who will offer you a solution instead of creating more problems.

Look for those who bring out the best in you, skip those who bring you more stress and drama.

Drama is not welcome anyway, especially not in those moments when you need your peace.

Those who can sit with you in your dark moments, those are keepers and those are the ones who deserve you!

And after the storm, don't forget those who have helped you by being there for you. Be grateful for having them in your life.

And be there for others too, bring a calm to someone's storm.

326

"We suffer more in imagination than in reality." - Lucius Annaeus Seneca

Very truuuue.

We can be our worst enemies. We are capable of creating a living hell and worst nightmares, just with our thoughts. This can be so exhausting.

We can imagine the worst-case scenarios in our heads and 99% of those things will never happen.

Also, we can suffer so much thinking what others think about us. Again, those thoughts usually aren't right.

Try to be your best friend and to choose your thoughts wisely, in order to avoid overthinking.

And If you want to know what other people think of you, just ask them. Let's say something happened that caused awkward situation between the two of you. Don't assume. Ask. Always ask. Even if your assumption was correct, still ask them to see what they have to say. Just don't make decisions based on your assumptions, you should have a clear picture instead.

Thus, ask, talk. Break that chain reaction of "negative" thoughts, or better to say, thoughts that don't serve you at all.

327

"Is showing emotion a sign of weakness or strength?"

Since when has this been questioned?

The answer is very clear and without a doubt: showing emotions is a sign of STRENGTH!

It takes true courage to open yourself to someone.

It takes true courage to tell someone you like or love them, regardless the answer.

It takes true courage to express how you feel.

It takes true courage to show your vulnerability.

It takes true courage to say when you get hurt.

It takes true courage to show your pain.

It takes true courage to ask for help.

It takes true courage to show your tears to someone.

It takes true courage to love someone, but let them go.

It takes true courage TO BE REAL among people who wear masks.

It takes true courage to speak your mind, even though people will judge you.

It takes true courage to be honest in the world full of hypocrisy.

It's like being completely naked among people.

Don't let anyone ever tell you that you are weak for expressing how you feel. Stay away from them.

Be real. Keep it real. Find a way to say what's on your mind and heart, and don't ever regret for saying it, you can only regret for not staying true to yourself.

328

"Learn to wait. There is always time for everything."

To me one of the most difficult lessons to apply. Again, patience, one step at a time. Sometimes, change can't happen overnight.

Having patience and accepting the life as it is can be very difficult.

Especially when we lose someone. Especially when things don't go as we expect them to go.

Especially when things don't depend on us. And we want them to happen so badly, because we think we need them. And maybe something better is waiting for us out there, but we are attached so strongly to our wish, so we don't allow ourselves to think that there's something even better.

Let go of expectations and let the things flow.

The key is acceptance: it is how it is. Yes, it can be difficult, but is there any other option? I guess not.

Learning to accept things as they are and being grateful for what we have. At this exact moment. You never know what tomorrow holds.

And patience, in order to have inner peace.

Which is the most important thing. Yes, inner peace.

329

"I have no country to fight for; my country is the earth, and I am a citizen of the world." - Eugene V. Debs

We are all as one. We are all the same. Yet, we are all unique, we are all different. We are spiritual human beings.

Planet Earth is our home. We should focus more on protecting and taking care of our home instead of thinking about what religion we are.

Religion is invented by people to control the masses, to give "a reason" to people to hate each other, to start wars, to argue with each other, to die for interests of who knows who.

There is nothing wrong with believing. On the contrary. I even believe in unicorns. We live what we believe in and that's the point, to believe. Believe in yourself, your true-self. And take care of your home.

Be kind, respect others and LOVE. Give love so the love always comes back to you. Love is my religion.

330

"No one wants to support you at the start of your journey but once they see your success they all want to be friends again."

Ok, maybe not no one, but only a few.

People are too busy with their own shit, so, of course, that they have no time to support you.

But when you succeed, all of a sudden, they have time for you, to talk to you, to call you, to see how you are doing.

Isn't it strange? Naaah, it's not, it just speaks a lot about them. And this happens way too often.

The point is: If you can't handle me at my worst, if you don't support my idea, my work, my struggle, my sacrifice, then what makes you think you deserve me at my best? If you are not with me to help me while I'm begging, then don't expect me to let you in my world when I'm on the top.

Of course, they will expect it no matter what, because they need you. But remember that those people aren't loyal to you, but to their need of you.

Think a bit, just think about it, it's not that difficult.

And don't touch my aura with your dirty hands.

331

"Abandonment Issues – I always wondered why it was so easy for people to leave. What I should have questioned was why I wanted so badly for them to stay."

A very good perspective!

If they want to leave, let them leave!

No one should be a prisoner.

Maybe you see something they don't see and you can't force them to see that if they are "blind".

Nowadays, in my opinion, commitment is one of those things that is really rare to see. People give up so easily. The bump into the first obstacle and boom – they give up.

Especially when it comes to relationships.

What happens next, instead of leaving completely, both physically and mentally, they stay physically in relationships while mentally they are somewhere else. Especially when you add all the distractions we have today, with internet and one-click-escape.

But in the end, it's all about self-respect.

Respect yourself enough to let go of anyone who wants to leave! So, if they want to leave, hold the door open for them... on their way out!

And wait for those who want to commit to a relationship. To build it and nurture it.

332

"Staying positive doesn't necessarily mean being happy all the time. It just means that even when you're feeling low, you know that it will end, and that there are better days on the other side."

I really, madly, deeply dislike when people confuse being positive with being "happy" all the time!

You know what, shit happens to everybody! The difference is how you deal with it.

Being positive means staying strong even when everything falls apart.

My very essence is positive. Sometimes, I hear people tell me: oh, it's easy for you ($@#*?#)... At that moment, I would give them all my shit to deal with. Oh, how I wish I could. Maybe they could learn something from it.

You can't even imagine what kind of a hurricane such nonsense creates within me. I can feel the steam coming out from my ears.

Well, back then, I was just like that. Now I know that only people who play a role of victim have that kind of mindset: poor me, it's easy for you. They blame everything/everyone else instead of taking responsibility for their lives.

So, I try to step away and not get involved in their dramas.

If I don't complain it doesn't mean I have no problems. I do have them, we all do, but the difference is in our mindset. I know that speaking about problems won't help me! I rather speak about solutions!

Stop complaining & do something, like changing your MINDSET! If you can't change your life's situation, you CAN change how to deal with it! And stop spreading your "poor me" shit attitude around.

333

"You know the truth by the way it feels."

Oh, we all know the truth. Energy never lies.

The thing is that very often people choose to ignore it.

But deep inside, we all know the truth by the way it feels.

Why people choose to ignore the truth?

By doing this, you are lying to yourself. That way, you show NO respect for yourself.

Energy never lies. We can even recognize when others lie to us. When people we know well lie to us, we can almost feel it. So why do people accept lies?

They deny the obvious signals (the gut feeling), looking for excuses to justify themselves for accepting the lies.

And they continue to live a lie.

Or...

Signs of self-love and self-respect are when you accept the truth no matter how hard it is. Take responsibility for your life.

If someone lies to you, you can choose to listen to your gut feeling and require the truth.

Accept and confront the situation.

It's up to you.

You can't live your life denying the obvious. I mean, of course you can, lots of people live that way.

But please don't be 'lots of people'.

334

"You never know what someone else is going through. Be kind. Always."

Do you like when people treat you with respect and kindness? Well, I hope you treat them the same way.

Being kind to yourself and to others costs nothing, it should be part of your education. And to someone, maybe, it means everything.

We never know what someone else is going through, regardless of how much money they make or the great life you think they're living. But we can make a huge difference simply by being kind.

335

"Emotional pain cannot kill you but running from it can. Allow. Embrace. Let yourself feel. Let yourself heal." – Vironika Tugaleva

There is nothing wrong with being sad or angry. We are all humans, not robots, and life surprises us with various different situations.

Remember that:

We need to live by following our feelings! If you need to cry... CRY. Do you suppress yourself from laughing? DON'T.

Very often people try not to think about pain by being busy. Being occupied with so many things, but themselves.

Work can help us, so we don't overthink. But escaping from your feelings won't help you, it can actually be self-destructive. And self-destruction leads to pfff...

Let me give you an example: people who drink too much, do drugs, eat too much etc. The reason behind all that is what makes a difference. The reason should be joy, not escape, thinking that your feelings will disappear. Well they won't. Any kind of addiction is not fun. It's a consequence of the accumulation of shit people avoid to deal with. Frustrations. Escaping from the pain is the cause of any addiction!

Give yourself time to process, to "digest" life's situations.

Find someone you can talk to, but most importantly, have a self-talk. Find the cause of your pain and take your time to heal. Embrace, love and connect with yourself, but never escape from how you feel! You can't escape yourself. Ne-va'.

336

"We don't like to read and understand. But we love to comment. That's us." - Erykah Badu

Lots of people don't like to listen with intention to understand.

They listen just to reply.

Lots of people don't want to learn how to listen to other people's experiences.

They listen so they can speak about their own stuff afterwards.

Lots of people don't like to read and understand what they read. For instance, motivational quotes.

But they do like expressing their opinions.

About everything. About everyone.

And that's ok, that's ok, we all have opinions. But your opinion will only matter if it's based on your knowledge, if you know what you're talking about.

Otherwise, what's the point? It's like listening to some noise. Blah blah blah...

I know they are not aware of this. If they are, they would not say things without thinking about them in the first place.

Stay away from me. Oh, no, you already have an opinion about me, without even knowing me.

And that's ok, that's ok, we all have opinions about others. Just make sure that you do not look at the others through your eyes, from your perspective. If you really want to know them. If you want to know yourself, then yes, what you see in them, speaks about you.

Step back intruders, don't touch my aura.

337

"Doing as others told me, I was Blind. Coming when others called me, I was Lost. Then I left everyone, myself as well. Then I found Everyone, Myself as well." – Rumi

The more I find myself, the more people lose me.

The more I know myself, the less I care about other people's opinion.

The more I understand myself, the more I understand others.

The more aware I become, the less I need approval from others.

The more I respect myself, the more selective I become.

The more I believe in myself, the less I need others to believe in me.

The more I learn, the more I see how little I know.

The more I love myself, the more...

338

"You'll find another.' God! Banish the thought. Why don't you tell me that 'if the girl had been worth having, she'd have waited for you'? No, sir, the girl really worth having won't wait for anybody." - F. Scott Fitzgerald

No sir, the girl really worth having, won't wait for anybody!

What makes you think that she is going to wait for someone who has no guts to make a simple decision?

Sir, the girl really worth having doesn't need you.

She wants you.

Spot the difference.

Thus, remind me again, what makes you so special that you think that she would be waiting for you?

So, sir, if you have some guts, go and get her!

If she is really worth having go and get her!

Don't give another man an opportunity to make your woman smile!

And, sir, if you have no guts, just don't stand at the door, you're blocking the traffic.

339

"Be happy, you never know how much time you have left!"

Do all those things that make you feel happy, no matter how scary it sounds, it is the truth: you never know what tomorrow brings!

You don't even know what may happen within one hour, all you have is now.

Live your life in the way you want to live it, do things that make your heart jump in joy.

Make memories, the valuable ones. You know, in life, little things matter the most. Simple, small things that make life sooo big!

Because at the end, all old people say the same things, that they've spent so much time worrying what other people will think. They always regret the chances and risks they didn't take to live a better life, to choose a better partner, to say how they feel etc.

Knowing this, instead of waiting the end or to get old, saying the same things, let's skip that step and apply this wisdom now. Because, you really don't know what tomorrow holds.

Message him, call her out, say how you feel, connect with people who are good for your soul, book that trip, explore, learn how to play guitar, dance, dance in the rain, do something good every day, for you and for the others...

And love! Love a lot!

340

"Sometimes people don't want to hear the truth because they don't want their illusions destroyed." - Friedrich Nietzsche

I'm not here to tell you what you would like to hear.

I'm not writing with intention to support unhappy lives. Lost dreams.

I'm not here to support your illusions.

I'm not here to be loved or liked.

I'm not here to preach you how you should live your life.

I'm not one of those copy/paste speakers.

Neither a life coach. Your life is your only coach.

The reason why I have my blog and why I write my articles is NOT to gain followers or to write things you would like to read.

I'm writing because I love it.

I'm sharing my life with intention to wake up those who want to be awakened.

I put myself and my soul out there.

I'm doing it because there are so many things I need to say, for myself and to help you.

I am here to speak my truth.

To motivate you, talking about my experiences.

My beliefs and values.

My intention is to make you think.

My intention is to shake you, your world, your beliefs and remind you that there is only 1 life.

The same thing I do to me.

Whether you like it or don't, either way, great.

I'll keep speaking my mind with my heart no matter what you think about it.

I don't care about opinions, the only thing I care about is whether I can help someone.

"I have struggled in ways no one knows about, it has made me stronger, confident and fearless. And no one can take that away from me."

When we struggle, we either overcome it and become stronger or we become weak – the victims.

All those struggles I had have shaped me and "forced" me to grow. Or I forced myself to grow.

My personality, my integrity – my values. My understanding of life. Knowledge. Many other things too.

All decisions I had to make, experiences I had, have made me and who I'm today.

All those situations in life I had to overcome. Alone. It was painful. It was difficult. But giving up wasn't an option. For me.

I try to do what's right, not easy. Because integrity and true values are things I nurture deep within.

And no one can take that away from me. Ne-va'.

I feel very grateful. If life was easier on me, I wouldn't be so strong.

Please, never be ashamed of your feelings. Never be afraid to admit that you struggle. We all struggle. But you decide for yourself.

Your past decisions have made you who you are today.

Thus, decisions you make today will determine your tomorrow!

Don't be afraid of life. Be aware that you are the creator of your life by making decisions. If you are not in charge of what life brings you, you are in charge of your decisions. That way you shape yourself and your life.

342

"It was a man who changed my perception completely that men are loving, caring and damn loyal too." – Suri Singh

Of course, they exist! I know they do...

How beautiful is to have a man who treats you right. Oh man, loyalty is sooo attractive. RESPECT & Intelligence too.

A man who knows how to take care of you. Who loves you in the way that will make you feel safe, who looks at you like you're the most beautiful living creature on earth. His "one and only". Priceless. Keepers.

I know they are rare, those loving, caring men with integrity, but I assure you they do exist. That's what make them so special and unique.

When a man loves a woman...

If you say they don't exist, I disagree. Know that you live what you believe in. What you give, you will receive. What you allow it will reach you.

Of course, the same applies for women as well.

343

"When I loved myself enough, I began leaving whatever wasn't healthy. This meant people, jobs, my own beliefs and habits – anything that kept me small. My judgement called it disloyal. Now I see it as self-loving." – Kim McMillen, When I Loved Myself Enough

Very true! When you learn to love yourself unconditionally you will start to change, logically. Your consciousness as well.

You will learn to respect yourself, you will start to re-question your beliefs. To create the new ones, which will truly serve you.

You will let go of anything that kept you small, that "forced" you to shrink so you could adjust to your surroundings.

You will start being more honest with yourself. Your mind and thoughts will be clearer, about what to do to feel in peace with yourself.

You will raise your standards, and of course, you will start letting go of anything that doesn't feel right. Your closest friends. Even family. Your partner.

Change won't be easy, but it's extremely important to do the right thing! It's like a never-ending process. Because we change all the time. What today feels good for you, tomorrow may not feel the same.

Remember...

The only person that stops from loving yourself and listening to yourself (your true self) is the one you see in the mirror!

344

"Never run back to whatever broke you."

For your own sake! Remember yourself how much time you needed to heal?

If you think they've changed... think again. Just don't run back, but observe.

Know that: You can't "help" others – unless they want to be

"helped". That's their job. And your job is to help yourself instead of putting yourself through the same shitty situation that was painful for you. You decide. This time, it would be your conscious decision.

And if you feel lonely, again, you should help yourself. And going back to whatever broke you isn't the help you need.

Be your own hero. We all are our own heroes. At least, we should be.

Think about yourself, love yourself.

Because you know what: you are the one with whom you will spend the rest of your life. So be your best friend. Thus, wouldn't you give the same advice to your best friend?

Be kind. To yourself in the first place.

345

"Ignorance brings chaos, not knowledge." – Lucy (2014)

"The world is a dangerous place to live; not because of the people who are evil, but because of the people who don't do anything about it." – Albert Einstein

"Knowledge is power, but the power of ignorance has no limits." – Myself

Oh, I feel so wise today.

346

"To Men: Never take a good woman for granted because one day another guy will come along and appreciate what you didn't."

... and vice versa. The point is: It is all about appreciation and respect for both women or men.

Some people won't start appreciating you until they lose you.

Being aware of this, once again, we can skip this step and start appreciating people we love.

Maybe you think you do appreciate them, but somehow you have forgotten to show that to them.

Love is not something implied just by being in a relationship, love should be shown! By taking care of them. Love can be shown in so many ways, and no, I don't mean to say: I love you. Those are just words.

The loneliest people I know are actually in relationships.

So if you love your partner, let's start by telling them how much they mean to you. They should feel your words. That you are grateful for having them in your life. Ask them if they are happy with you, connect with them. Etc.

Of course, if you don't love them, if you don't mean what you say, what's the point? Go where the love is, as you both deserve love. Your effort shows your interest. Your effort reflects intentions. Just as no effort reflects your intentions.

Make her/him yours or watch how someone else appreciates them instead..

347

"It's rare to find someone who is not full of shit these days."

But you know, almost everyone is pretending to be "happy".

"How are you?"

"Great, the job is great, everything is great."

Five minutes later, you start a fight with someone out of the blue.

Are you sure that you are feeling great?

Just look around you or within you. People passing their frustrations to one another as if that's something natural.

Because someone taught us we should always say we are feeling good, when the question 'how are you' pops out.

I'm not saying that you should go around complaining, but be honest with yourself first. We are all full of shit.

Some people choose to deal with difficult situations and others don't. They rather ignore it instead of dealin' with it. Yeah, let's hide the shit under the rug, because that's the solution. No one will notice it. But you. And it will keep getting bigger.

Let's try to be kind one to another.

I am, but I won't take any shit from anyone. Not anymore. You can be sure about that. I'll give it back to you as a gift with a bow. Because your trash doesn't belong to me.

Neither to anyone. Deal with your own shit instead of having a false happy-go-lucky attitude, screaming for help from within.

348

"Stop wishing your life was different and live the one you have because it's the only one you've got."

In case you wish the things you cannot possibly have, to have a life you don't live, or to be someone else, how long will you keep doing this to yourself?

Don't you think that it's just a waste of your time? You can't swap your life for someone else's. You can't be someone else. You simply can't. Accept that fact.

So stop wasting your precious time.

You've got your life to live, so live it to the fullest!

Instead of putting your focus on what you don't have, try to count all those things you have. You would be surprised how many things you have to be grateful for. Things we usually take for granted.

Then, find a way to make your life better instead of bitter and do it. Concentrate on yourself, and your life.

... and please do not compare yourself to others, NE-VA'! Grass is greener on the other side of the fence because you have forgotten to nurture your own.

Mindset, oh, that mindset.

349

"You are the books you read, the films you watch, the music you listen to, the people you meet, the dreams you have, the conversations you engage in. You are what you take from these."

If we know that we are the creators of our lives by making decisions...

We decide how we will spend the time that is given to us. We decide whether we are going to participate in something we don't feel good about or not. And, simply by following our gut feeling, we will know what's good for us.

Are you a type of person who would go out just because

someone else insists? Maybe someone you don't even like? Will you go to a party even if you would rather stay home in your pyjamas reading a book? Do you participate in conversations you don't want to, gossiping?

If you do any of these, ask yourself: Why? You know that it's your right to say NO to anything that you don't feel good about? Are you aware that by saying yes to others you said no to yourself, not showing any respect to yourself? If you don't respect yourself how can you expect respect from others?

Would you rather please others, even if that means betraying yourself in order to be liked and accepted? Again, why?

Do you think that you are a good person by doing it? Nope, this doesn't mean you are a good person! Especially not if you are gossiping.

Self-acceptance is far more important than acceptance from others. Do things you really love and surround yourself with people you enjoy spending time with.

350

"You gotta know the difference between being patient & wasting your time."

Sometimes, it can be really hard to tell with whom you want to go through the storm to see the rainbow and the sun, and who you need to let go of just because they can be toxic for you.

For instance...

We all go through life dealing with different stuff. Sometimes, you will meet someone you really like, and at that point they might face some difficulties. If you really like them, help them go through that just by being there for them. Patience. Don't give up on them just because they are not at their best. Would you like people giving up on you when you struggle? Keep this in mind.

On the other hand, some people are not sure how they feel about you, sending you mixed signals – one day they are there for you, the other day you don't even hear from them. You can't force anyone or anything… rather let them go.

You gotta know when to hold on to them, when to walk or run away from them, you just gotta know.

Thanks to you experiences and learning from them, you are able to follow your heart and intuition. It's much easier to spot that difference simply by how you feel, because of – energy? Energy never lies.

351

"Never apologize to others for their misunderstanding of who you are."

If you apologize to others for who you are, this means that you are not happy with who you are!

Always apologize when you make a mistake or when you are wrong. When you hurt someone.

But to apologize for being yourself? Pleeeeeeease, neva' but neva' do that!

I repeat NEVA'!

It means that you are ashamed of who you are! Are you?

Apologize to yourself for trying to please others and stay away from people who simply can't accept the way you are.

We are all different, and we should accept others as they are the same way we should be accepted from others for who we are.

It's like apologising for existing. For breathing.

This doesn't mean that we are perfect.

This means that we are aware of ourselves and who we are, always working on ourselves to be better humans. At least I hope that people work on themselves to be better than who they were yesterday.

This means we are unique and that's our power.

And don't forget this: we don't see others as they are, but as we are. So remind me again, to apologize for what?

352

"Stay away from people that make you feel you are hard to love."

Speaking about personalities, if you feel different, or that you don't fit in the box, please don't you dare think that you are hard to love or that you are too much or whatever else people might say to you.

You are who you are. Get to know yourself and make sure that you don't look at yourself through their eyes.

Most people tend to categorise you or to put some label on you, just because they don't understand you.

Being different doesn't mean that you're good or bad. But it's easier to say, oh, he/she is crazy, stay away from them, than to try to understand them. And learn something new. But, oh, who has the time to learn new things.

Judging is not something you need in your life. To be judged or to judge others.

The most important thing is: be sure that you're not one of those people who tells anyone they are hard to love. Maybe you're hard to love or maybe you're not capable to love them in the right way. So instead of judging, let them go.

Everything is always vice versa. When you point a finger at others you have three fingers pointing back.

Thus, if you are saying that someone is too deep, you're telling yourself that you're too shallow. Superficial.

353

"You can't change other people you can only change yourself. when you change yourself, the people that creating issues in your life either change with you or go away. When you shift, everything around you shifts."

Change starts with ourselves.

You can't change others, neither you should! You should accept them as they are.

First of all, you should be yourself, accepting yourself as you are.

Change starts with a simple decision, even the smallest one that will bring you one step closer to your inner peace.

In that process of changing, you give example to others that they can change too. It's up to them whether they want to grow and change with you or stay where they are. But they will notice it, and usually they will "complain" how you've changed (Those who stay just where they are).

This shouldn't bother you as it's your life. You are the only one responsible for your life and your happiness. You should tell them: thank you, I know I'm. For the better. People usually complain when you stop living up to their expectations, but remember this is your life we talk about.

In the next step, you will start to letting go of people, even the closest ones, or they will "remove" themselves from your life. But, you will start attracting like-minded people or those who are on the same journey experiencing similar situation. That's the beauty of the process.

As you can see... Change starts with you! Then everything around you will change.

354

"What you can't say owns you. What you hide controls you."

Finding inner peace is something we should always strive for.

And avoiding your life is not a proper way to achieve this.

You will never be able to escape yourself. Ne-va'. You can avoid life, people, situations, you can even move to another country, but you will never be able to avoid yourself.

Suppressing your emotions can lead to self-destruction. To the emptiness from within.

You will drag around all those unprocessed thoughts, unspoken feelings, painful situations within yourself wherever you go. And you should really get rid of that burden.

Facing life situations and accepting the life as such is crucial.

There is one sentence that I struggled to accept without asking million questions (and not to get pissed off when I hear it). But, if you understand it properly, it can bring you immense peace, so here we go: You're exactly where you need to be.

A great starting point, don't you think?

Thus, it's better to listen to your life, some message out there is waiting for you...

355

"I know, I'm leaving you with your worst enemy. Yourself."
– Louis Malle's "The Fire Within", 1963

I know, but sorry-not-sorry. I can't be your therapist. I've learnt that lesson a long time ago.

And, I love to feel connected in a relationship.

But if people don't learn how to be independent, if they don't spend some time on their own, to learn how to love themselves, they will always depend on others in relationships.

Just to make myself clear, I don't talk about economic but emotional independence.

If you don't work on yourself, you will always have certain expectations from your partner. To be your saviour. To be your escape. To take the role of your mother/father. Your therapist.

And none of this should be your partner. Your partner is not there to entertain you, neither to teach you what responsibility is.

You should learn that everything we look for is not in others, but within us. So instead of torturing others with your expectations, and passing on them your frustrations, try to work on yourself.

When you learn how to be happy on your own, how to love

yourself you will be ready to give/receive love.

You will be ready to connect in the right way, to love your partner for who they are, not because you need them.

Two independent people who are connected to each other because they want each other, not because they need each other.

356

"It's not your fault. Sometimes, brave women fall in love with cowards."

It's not your fault! First of all, falling in love is not a bad thing! It is a beautiful feeling.

And you are beautiful because you are capable of loving and not being afraid to show your love. Darling, that is very a brave thing to do in this world. BUT if he behaved cowardly, let him go.

And vice versa.

You don't want a coward. You want someone who will be there for you. As you are there for them. Someone who will stick by your side, in good and bad times. Someone who will hold your hand decisively and proudly.

To love is the prerogative of the brave ones. A coward is incapable of loving others. So do yourself a favour and let them go.

People struggle to love themselves. Don't you dare think that you have made some mistake. Make sure you put a full stop when you see that the love you give is not appreciated. No comma, no question mark, but a full stop.

357

"Learn the difference between connection and attachment. Connection gives you power, Attachment sucks the life out of you."

Speaking about any kind of relationships, are you connected to your partner/friend or attached for some reason (in need)? Is your partner connected or attached to you?

You will know by the way you feel. Drained? Content?

Try not to confuse attachment with love.

Attachment is all about dependency, fears. It has more to do with needing someone, which means more self-love (egoism) than loving someone else.

When you love someone, you love them for who they are, and they feel free around you. There is no attachment, but commitment. Connection.

HUGE difference.

358

"Just because a decision hurts that doesn't mean it was a wrong decision."

Do what is right, not what is easy.

Waiting hurts.

Leaving hurts.

Letting go hurts.

Moving on hurts.

Breaking up hurts.

Divorcing hurts.

Forgiving hurts.

But...

Nothing hurts more than staying somewhere you don't belong to.

Nothing hurts more than staying with someone you don't love.

Nothing hurts more than pretending that you're happy, when you are falling apart within.

You decide.

We should be making decisions based on what feels right for us. For all. Those decisions lead to change. Changes, very often, are not easy. But necessary. Thus, do what is right, not what is easy. That means having integrity.

Sometimes you need to fall apart so you can put yourself back together. That's when growth is happening. That's what strength is, and in case that you don't remember, I'll remind you that you're strong enough and you will survive changes.

359

"When people walk away from you, let them go. You shouldn't have to talk them into staying with you, loving you, calling you, caring about you, and coming to see you, because if they really cared about you, in the first place, they would not be going anywhere."

If something isn't given freely... let that shit go! If you have to force something, leave it.

If you have any self-respect and if you love yourself, chasing or begging are not the options. You will know that staying in an unhealthy relationship can only stop you from finding your own peace, your own path. Your growth.

Definitely, they've been part of your life for some reason, but it doesn't mean that they should stay there forever.

If they leave you, this doesn't mean that they are good or bad, it simply means that it is pointless to force something that doesn't flow naturally.

Remember, the same way you walked out from someone's life. So accept their decision the same way you would like that other people to accept your decision to walk out from their life.

And It's not about those who leave you, but about those who stay.

Know that there are right things and people waiting for you somewhere, be sure about it! They are waiting to step IN your life. Just don't beg, don't chase ANYONE. Please.

Thus, if people walk away... let them walk.

360

"Remember: Just because you went to college doesn't make you smarter than anyone else, Common sense doesn't come with a degree."

A lack of common sense affects the world. We can see it on daily basis.

Something we don't learn in the school although it is essential. How to use common sense? We all have it, but lots of people don't use it. Sadly.

Actually, you don't even need a school for that. We all have ability to make a distinction between right and wrong. Maybe people need to be reminded that common sense is given freely and they shouldn't be afraid of using it.

Your diploma won't make you a good person, but using common sense will.

Education without common sense can be lethal.

361

"The opinion which other people have of you is their problem, not yours." - Elisabeth Kubler-Ross

1. What other people think of you, how they see you, speaks more about themselves.

Therefore, what you think of others and how you perceive others speaks more about yourself.

2. What other people think of you is none of your business.

Therefore, what you think of other people is none of their business.

Live and let live. And love.

Remember:

When you judge others you don't define them, but yourself.

Namaste.

362

"Of course, I am not worried about intimidating men. The type of man who will be intimidated by me is exactly the type of man I have no interest in." – Chimamanda Ngozi

Oh, STRENGTH is soooo attractive. I know. We all want that one who is strong enough, because they give us the feeling of a safe place, someone we can lean on. Someone who will lead the way when we can't.

The question is, how strong are you?

The thing is that strong minds will attract strong minds or offend the weak ones.

In any sphere of life, any kind of relationship.

How strong can you be if the strength of one woman intimidates you? Her mental strength. Her mind. Her vision.

If someone intimidates you, try asking yourself: "Why am I intimidated by her, him, boss or anyone?"

I had to learn this the hard way. Oh, what happens is that the weak people who are afraid of my strength try to drag me down just because they feel insecure in their own skin. And they are attracted to me in the first place because of my strength. But their insecurities and fears take them over.

If I feel intimidated by someone, I always ask myself why? And if the answer is *because of his strength,* then I see that as an opportunity for me to grow. And I love it!

I'm definitely not worried or interested in men who are intimidated by me. And trust me, so many of them are. They are exactly what I don't want in my life.

Taa-daaah!

363

"It's rare to meet someone with a mind just as beautiful as their face."

We live in a world where people judge you based on your appearance and where perfect body is "a must have". Whatever that perfect means.

They put labels on you: fat, skinny, anorexic, you should be eating less/more... Listening to all of that can be really painful.

That's the reason why lots of people want "perfect bodies". The fact is they just want to be accepted. Yet, very few of them openly speak about it. Like I do.

They will suffer & develop diseases just to look good: go through never-ending aesthetic surgeries/treatments, anorexia, bulimia, body dysmorphia, not thinking about their health, but about their appearance.

The reason why is what makes a difference. Do you want a nice fit body because you want to be healthy and happy or because you feel under pressure watching Instagram photos and YouTube videos of perfectly shaped bodies?

The consequence of all this is that people don't pay attention to their bodies. From within. Their soul and their essence thus suffer. They become unhappy, striving to satisfy others in order to be accepted, at the same time forgetting about the self-acceptance.

We have so many beautiful bodies walking around, yet being so empty from within.

It's really rare to find someone with a mind and soul just as beautiful as their face. Physical beauty fades away, but inner beauty NEVER does.

364

"I have decided to stick with love. Hate is too great a burden to bear." – Martin Luther King, Jr.

Life lessons. One of the hardest one for me for so many reasons: Forgiveness. Forgiving someone who has hurt me. Oh, boy.

I think we all go around hurting each other on daily basis without even being aware of it.

But I'm not talking about that. I'm talking about those who did you wrong. Maybe someone who lied about you, or to you or who has on you. You know, any type of situation that caused you to suffer. When you felt strong pain and sadness. Even depression. First of all, know this, your suffering won't hurt them back, it will only hurt yourself even more.

The inability to forgive is actually hurting you. That's why the importance of forgiveness is immense.

I don't mean you should put on your happy-go-lucky attitude and continue your life by ignoring them.

I'm just saying, take your time.

Forgiveness doesn't mean your approval. Forgiving doesn't mean justifying bad behaviour.

Forgiving means that you understand the situation. You accept it. Forgiving means maturity. Forgiving means controlling your ego. Forgiveness means STRENGTH.

And... Forgiving doesn't mean you want them back! Hell, no.

Forgive them for your own inner peace. You deserve peace. Forgiving means allowing yourself to heal. Forgiving means taking care of you and your health.

Accept And Forgive. Let it go. And... love. Love heals.

365

What would you do if there was no tomorrow?

366

"I might not tell you this enough, but I appreciate you being in my life."

So very much...

Don't take people you love for granted, you never know what tomorrow brings.

Tell them you love them, just how much you appreciate them, how much you care for them. Let your heart speaks, forget about the ego games, forget about the fear, because tomorrow might be late. To love is to give! Like I give myself here.

Me... I'm going to tell my special ones how much I care for them. What about you?

I don't know you at all, but I appreciate you very much! Your thank-you messages, your respect, your appreciation, your comments, your strength, your persistence, your changes. I'm growing and learning thanks to you too. Thank you for being here and making my blah blah blah stories very important. We are all connected. I don't know you, but I love you...

ABOUT ME..

So, let me introduce myself. My name is Irina Vujaklija and I was born in Belgrade on 31 January 1979.

Discovering my true self wasn't an easy process. Constantly working on myself, learning by seeking answers to many questions, I have managed to overcome some very complicated life situations. Among other things, my severe motorcycle accident in 2004, a life altering moment in just one second. Followed by 11 surgeries. Twice doctors have fought to save my life.

I was lost.. so, I had to find myself.

I had so many questions.. I had so many feelings, emotions and situations I didn't know how to handle, so I had to learn the hard way.

That's how my writing began. That's why I have the need to share with you all my secrets of overcoming very challenging life situations. To help you. Because sharing is caring, and caring is love. I don't know you, but I love you, and I wish you to be free, to feel free, to think free and to be responsible for your life.

Love,

Irina Vujaklija

You can find me on social media: A Thinking Bond Blonde